Just as phys. science is ~~crude~~ expose
of ideal, conversely Word expresses
higher order spiritual relation of Univ.
& God.

DIVINE
AND CONTINGENT ORDER

DIVINE
AND
CONTINGENT
ORDER

THOMAS F. TORRANCE

Nihil constat de
contingentia
nisi ex revelatione

OXFORD NEW YORK TORONTO MELBOURNE
OXFORD UNIVERSITY PRESS
1981

Oxford University Press, Walton Street, Oxford OX2 6DP

London Glasgow New York Toronto
Delhi Bombay Calcutta Madras Karachi
Kuala Lumpur Singapore Hong Kong Tokyo
Nairobi Dar es Salaam Cape Town
Melbourne Wellington
and associate companies in
Beirut Berlin Ibadan Mexico City

Published in the United States by
Oxford University Press, New York

British Library Cataloguing in Publication Data

Torrance, Thomas F.
Divine and contingent order.
1. Creation   2. Theology, Doctrinal
I. Title
233'.1   BT695
ISBN 0-19-826658-8

Set by Hope Services, Abingdon
and printed in Great Britain by
Billing & Sons Ltd,
Guildford, London & Worcester

To
E.L. Mascall and S.L. Jaki,
and in memory of
Georges Florovsky,
champions of contingence,
in deep appreciation

Preface

If we are asked what we mean by speaking of events as 'contingent', we say 'they just happen to be like that'. There is more to it than this, however, for contingent events have an elusive character which we indicate by adding 'but they did not have to be like that, for they might have been very different'. It is in this fuller sense that the terms 'contingent' and 'contingence' are used in theology and in science, where they are applied not only to what things happen to be but to the kind of order or pattern they happen to have.

In the history of thought this fuller sense was bound up with the Judaeo-Christian conception that God freely created the universe out of nothing. This does not mean that he created it out of some stuff called 'nothing', but that what he created was not created out of anything. To think of the universe as having been brought into being in this way is to hold that the universe has been given a distinctive existence of its own, utterly different from God's. We describe it as contingent for it depends on God entirely for its origin and for what it continues to be in its existence and its order. The baffling thing about the creation is that since it came into being through the free grace of God it might not have come into being at all, and now that it has come into being it contains no reason in itself why it should be what it is and why it should continue to exist. Indeed God himself was under no necessity to create the universe. This is the way Duns Scotus once expressed it: 'The creation of things proceeds from God not out of any necessity whether of being or of knowledge or of will but out of pure freedom which is not moved, much less necessitated, by anything outside of itself so as to be brought into operation.' (*Quaestiones disputatae de rerum principio*, q.4, a.1, n.3)

By contingence is meant, then, that as created out of nothing the universe has no self-subsistence and no ultimate stability of its own, but that it is nevertheless endowed with an authentic reality and integrity of its own which must be respected. By contingent order is meant that the orderly universe is not self-sufficient or ultimately self-explaining but is given a rationality and reliability in its orderliness which depend on and reflect God's own eternal rationality and reliability. There is no doubt, as modern research has made very clear, that modern empirical science owes its existence to the injection of these notions of contingence and contingent order into the basic stock of ideas in our understanding of nature. It is also clear, however, that they took a long time to germinate and mature in such a way as to make it possible for the vast enterprise of experimental inquiry and discovery to get off the ground. The general effect of the Judaeo-Christian view of creation was to restore confidence in the rational integrity and authentic reliability of the world of nature which had been depreciated by ancient science and the long tradition of Augustinian culture, and to set nature free from the arbitrary necessities and timeless patterns imposed on it. It was only when it was understood to have a distinctive lawfulness of its own that nature was allowed to be really natural and to supply out of its own inner form rational evidence for scientific reasoning.

My main intention in writing this book is to clarify these notions of contingence and contingent order in the context of modern thought, and thereby to carry forward the work of early Christian theology which first injected these revolutionary ideas into the foundations of Western culture. In the early centuries of the Christian era this involved a profound struggle with the classical forms of thought prevailing in Graeco-Roman culture. In modern times contingence and contingent order have not had an easy passage either, owing in part to the persistence of ancient modes and methods of thought deriving from the Greeks, and in fact they have often been heavily overlaid and obscured by the elaboration of necessary patterns of thought, although they have nevertheless remained to constitute the very basis of our on-going empirico-theoretical science. Today, however, through the sheer rigour of scientific inquiry contingence and contingent order are once more being forced back into the material content of natural knowledge, where they demand to be treated, not merely as hidden presuppositions without which there would be no empirical science, but as essential factors in the regular understanding and interpreting of the natural order.

The history of thought has steadily reinforced the realization that, in spite of being necessary for natural science,
neither contingence nor contingent order can be demonstrated
by natural scientific operations, for they have to be assumed
in them all. They derive from outside of natural science,
from Christian theology. Thus both natural science and
theological science have a stake in these basic conceptions.
It is on this common ground that Christian theology, in
dialogue with natural science, needs to re-examine and
clarify the notion of creation, and that natural science, in
dialogue with Christian theology, can derive help for its
own difficult task as it pushes its investigations to the very
boundaries of being, to the very perimeter of the creation
of matter and form, where natural scientific modes and
formalizations of thought reach their limits. This book is
admittedly intended more for scientists than theologians,
and is offered to them in grateful acknowledgement of the
immense help I have derived from their brilliant and astonishing discoveries about the structures of created reality throughout the universe, in which I cannot but find ground for the
praise of the Creator and for continued support to faith. I
would hope, however, that theologians will also receive this
as an offering to them, with the prayer that it may stimulate
many of them to carry this kind of dialogue much further,
for I believe they will thereby gain a purified insight into
their own basic task of unfolding our human apprehension
of the Creator and Redeemer of the universe on the ground
of his active self-revelation to mankind.

The first three chapters of this book represent lectures I
have given to groups of scientists and theologians, and are
reproduced here with only subsidiary modification. 'Creation
and Determinism' was delivered to the International Institute
of Theoretic Sciences, combining the International Academies
of the Philosophy of Sciences and of Religious Sciences, at
its meeting in St. John's University, Long Island, New York,
on 9 July 1977. 'God and the Contingent World' was my
contribution to the Einstein celebrations held at Bern,
Switzerland, on 14 March 1979. And the third chapter,
under the title 'Divine and Contingent Order', in a somewhat
different form was the lecture delivered to the Oxford
International Symposium on 'The Sciences and Theology in

the Twentieth Century', at Christ Church, on 19 September
1979. The last chapter has been added in order to relate the
whole discussion to the difficult question of evil or disorder,
and to take up certain points that were omitted in the earlier
discussion. Each of the chapters can stand more or less on its
own, which means that there is some overlap in their content,
but they are intended to build up a progressive, if somewhat
spiral, argument.

This book is an essay in the tradition of Scottish realist
theological and epistemological thought which goes back at
least to John Duns Scotus. It was he who more than any
other in mediaeval times helped to recover the concepts of
contingence and contingent intelligibility after Neoplatonic
and Boethian thought had swamped them. It was Boethius
who first introduced the term *contingentia* into Western
vocabulary, but since it was his translation of an Aristotelian
notion, it was that concept of contingence rather than the
early Christian concept that prevailed in scholastic thought
until toward the end of the Middle Ages and the Reformation.
This book is also deeply indebted to the later tradition of
realist thought which through James Clerk Maxwell has
made such an epoch-making contribution to the revolution
in our understanding not only of physics but of the universe
itself, with which relativity, quantum and thermodynamic
theory are so closely related today. As I write this we are in
the midst of commemorating the centenary of the death of
James Clerk Maxwell, a great and humble man of science and
of faith for whom we give God thanks and praise.

To my dear wife, Margaret, I am more deeply indebted
than to any other in the things that matter most. Without her
unending love and patience and support I could do very
little, but with her, faith and joy in the love and beauty of
God are an increasing source of wonder and strength as we
grow older.

Edinburgh   THOMAS F. TORRANCE
5 Nov. 1979

Contents

Determinism and Creation

In natural science we are concerned ultimately, not with convenient arrangements of observational data which can be generalized into universal explanatory form, but with movements of thought, at once theoretical and empirical, which penetrate into the intrinsic structures of the universe in such a way that there becomes disclosed to us its basic design and we find ourselves at grips with reality. This has become increasingly evident since time as well as space became an inescapable ingredient in the subject-matter of science in our attempts to grasp the vectorial character of process and change within the moving system of the universe, for that raises with us questions of ultimate origins and ultimate ends. That is to say, we cannot pursue natural science scientifically without engaging at the same time in meta-scientific operations, not only at the meta-mathematical level but at the meta-physical level. The profounder our scientific inquiry into the universe, the more we are forced to grapple with cosmological questions and are committed to adopting a fundamental attitude to the universe as a whole, which affects fundamental theory and every theory-directed experiment. In theological science, on the other hand, we are concerned not just with relations between man and God but with the relationship of man in the universe to God the Creator of the universe, so that our understanding of the on-going universe itself cannot but enter into the coefficients of our theological statements, e.g. in their empirical correlates, not only when we are concerned specifically with creation and incarnation but also with every aspect of a theological account of God's interaction with us in the world where time and space constitute the orderly medium for divine revelation to man and human knowledge of God. Thus theological science, like natural science, cannot be pursued scientifically without being committed to a fundamental attitude to the universe, as it becomes disclosed to our understanding, and therefore without engaging in dialogue with natural science in the whole area of continuous time and space where their respective inquiries inevitably overlap and counter-questions have to be raised and answered.

An interconnection of this kind, deeply embedded in the teaching of the New Testament, came to the forefront in the development of classical Christian theology in the Nicene era as it struggled to break through the confusing identification of theology and cosmology that prevailed in contemporary Graeco-Roman culture. The distinctively Christian outlook upon the relation of God to the universe took shape as theologians thought through the bearing of the incarnation of the divine Logos in the spatial and temporal structures of created reality upon their understanding of the original creation of the universe out of nothing. One God, the Father Almighty, is the Creator of heaven and earth and of all things visible and invisible, while the incarnate Son or Logos, through whom all things were made and in whom they hold together, is the central and creative source of all order and rationality within the created universe. Far from being immanently bound up with the universe, God remains eternally and transcendently free, the absolute Lord over all space and time. Far from being a necessary emanation from the being of God, therefore, the universe is understood to have come into existence out of nothing freely through the will and power of God, as something utterly distinct from God and utterly dependent upon his ordering interaction with it. While the universe might have been other than it is, it came into being not without divine reason. Far from being merely an arbitrary product of God's will, the creation is regarded as having had its origin in the love of God and as ultimately grounded in the eternal truth and rationality of God. As such it remains utterly and continuously contingent upon the free creating power of God even in its creaturely truth and rationality.

There are three overlapping ideas here which are of relevance for our theme, for they have had considerable influence upon subsequent scientific and metaphysical, as well as theological, views of the universe and of the kind of order that prevails within it.

1. The doctrine of the One God, the Creator of all things

visible and invisible, and the ultimate source of all order and rationality, carried with it a rejection of the dualism, pluralism, and polymorphism of ancient philosophy, religion, and science, and thus gave rise to the conception of the universe as one harmonious system of things characterized by one pervasive if multi-variable order throughout. This rational unity of the cosmos, spanning celestial as well as terrestrial spheres, which is the correlate of Judaeo-Christian monotheism, has ever since constituted one of the fundamental assumptions of all science: it is the ground of our confidence that wherever we may direct our inquiries we will find the universe accessible to rational investigation and thought, even though, as correlated to the unlimited reality and rationality of God, the rationality of the universe has an indefinite range that reaches beyond the limits of our finite minds.

2. The infinite difference between the being of the Creator and the being of all created reality implies not only the rejection of the notion that God, even as First Cause, necessarily and logically belongs to what he has made, but also the all-important concept of contingent rationality inherent in created reality. The creation of the universe out of nothing involves the creation of space and time as well, which means that they are to be regarded as orderly features of empirical processes or events within the universe and not as detached empty 'containers'.[1] That is to say, space and time belong to the created order of things. However, the doctrine of creation also involves the idea that man himself, in mind as well as body, has been created out of nothing along with the universe, so that he is a constituent element in the created order of things as an essential ingredient in the complex of rational order intrinsic to the universe. The rationality of man and the rationality of the created universe belong inseparably together. Thus in creating the universe out of nothing God has conferred on it a created or contingent rationality of its own, as distinct from his divine rationality as creaturely being is from his divine being, yet as dependent on his uncreated rationality as creaturely being is upon his own being. Thus God has given contingent rationality within the universe a place and an authority which we are obliged to respect, not only if we are to have rational knowledge of

God through the medium of space and time where he com-
municates himself to us, but even if we are to investigate the
contingent processes of nature and discover their laws as far
as they may be disclosed to us. Here within the realm of
contingent events and contingent rationality we have to do
with connections which, precisely because they are contingent,
cannot be completely formalized, and so must guard against
the temptation through some sort of Euclidean idealization
to convert them into the kind of necessary connections which
we have in logico-causal relations. On the other hand, the
contingent rationality which pervades the created universe
demands a sufficient reason for the unitary order which
everywhere becomes manifest to our inquiries, but because
this rational order is contingent, and therefore not self-
sufficient, its sufficient reason becomes disclosed only
through correlation with some meta-level beyond it. Thus
if we are to take contingence seriously, without secretly
converting it into some kind of necessity, our scientific
inquiries and theories must operate with cross-level relations
between scientific and meta-scientific concepts, that is,
operate with reasons which cannot be reduced merely to
physical explanations.

3. The transcendence of God over all space and time
implies that the interaction of God with the universe he has
made rests on the free ground of his own eternal being. God
lives and acts in lordly freedom over all that is not God. His
creation of the universe out of nothing, however, far from
meaning that the universe is characterized by sheer necessity
either in its relation to God or within itself, implies that it is
given a contingent freedom of its own, grounded in the
transcendent freedom of God and maintained through his
free interaction with the universe. It was this doctrine of the
freedom of the creation contingent upon the freedom of
God which liberated Christian thought from the tyranny of
the fate, necessity, and determinism which for the pagan
mind was clamped down upon creaturely existence by the
inexorably cyclic processes of a self-sufficient universe.[2] Just
as there is an order in the universe transcendentally grounded
in God, so there is a freedom in the universe transcendentally
grounded in the freedom of God. However, just as order in
the universe is contingent, so the freedom in the universe is

contingent and therefore limited. Apart from being a self-contradiction, absolute freedom in contingency would not be freedom but an irrational arbitrariness. Freedom in the contingent universe is limited, but not less freedom because it is limited, for that which limits its freedom, the transcendent freedom of God, is the ground of its freedom as contingent. That is to say, limited freedom of this kind is the freedom proper to limited and contingent being, for it is inseparably bound up with its contingent rationality.[3]

It was in terms of these basic ideas that classical Christian theology of the fourth and fifth centuries set out to reconstruct the foundations of ancient philosophy and science upon which the pagan picture of God and the cosmos rested. Today we can see that they were masterful ideas which lay deep in the development of Western science, and with which we are more than ever concerned in the new science of our own day and its underlying concept of a unifying order. But what became of these ideas in thought subsequent to the Nicene and immediately post-Nicene era? For a short period they bore remarkable fruit in the physics of space and time, and of light and motion, that arose in Alexandria in the fifth and sixth centuries and which, like the theology out of which it grew, was thoroughly anti-dualist in its basic orientation. Before long, however, these ideas became swamped in the massive upsurge of dualist cosmologies and epistemologies which took somewhat different forms in the Augustinian West and the Byzantine East. The idea that the created universe is rational because its Creator and Preserver is rational remained, and was to see considerable development, especially in Western mediaeval theology and philosophy, which thus has contributed immensely to our scientific understanding of the universe. Unfortunately, however, the doctrine of God behind it all suffered not a little modification in terms of his inertial motion which was to have considerable effect upon classical Newtonian physics. Here the conception of the impassibility and immutability of God (i.e. that God is not subject to suffering or change), which has patristic sources, became allied to the Aristotelian notion of the Unmoved Mover. Although the idea of the creation of the universe out of nothing remained, that became difficult to maintain when the universe itself came

to be construed more and more in terms of Aristotle's four
causes in which the effect was understood as following
inexorably from its antecedent and defining cause, for to
regard the Creator as the First Cause from which the universe
took its rise appears to imply 'the eternity of the world' if
only in the mind of God who knows himself as its First
Cause. Mediaeval theology on evangelical grounds had to
reject the notion of 'the eternity of the world' but it remained trapped, for the most part at least, in notions of
impassibility and immutability of God which had as their
counterpart a notion of the world which, given its original
momentum by the First Cause, constituted a system of
necessary and causal relations in which it was very difficult
to find room for any genuine contingence. Contingence
could only be thought of in so far as there was an element
of necessity in it, so that contingence could be thought of
only by being thought away. The inertial relation of an
immutable God to the world he had made thus gave rise
to a rather static conception of the world and its immanent
structures. Looked at in this way it seems that the ground-
work for the Newtonian system of the world was already
to be found in mediaeval thought.

The concept of the impassibility and immutability of
God is actually ambiguous: it means that God is not moved
by anything outside of himself. He does not suffer from the
effect of anything other than God upon him; he is not moved
by any cause other than himself. In his eternal stability and
invariant reliability, he remains transcendent over all such
passion and change. But this does not mean that God does
not move himself, or that he is incapable of divine passion.
On the contrary, while God is serene and tranquil in the
face of any disturbance, trouble, or hurt that may arise in
the universe, he is nevertheless the living, self-moving God
who is in his own fullness a communion of love, who though
he is not eternally Creator was free to become the Creator
of all things visible and invisible. In the incarnation God
was free to do something new even for himself, for he was
not eternally incarnate, and free to move outside of himself
as he became incarnate, without being other than himself.
He is thus revealed as the God whose being is in his act and
whose act is in his being. This is the point which was originally

made by Athanasius when, thinking from a centre in the incarnation of God the Son in space and time, he claimed that, as the Logos revealed in the Son is internal to the being of God, so the act of God manifest in the work of the Son is internal to the being of God, for any separation between God's activity and his being would imply that God is not in himself what he is toward us through the Son and in the Spirit. The really decisive point for Athanasius is that in Jesus Christ it is God himself who has come among us savingly to make our existence and hurt his own, without ceasing to be what he is in his eternal reality. 'Thus it would appear that the question as to the impassibility of God is the question as to the actuality of the intersection of God's reality with worldly reality, and as to the depth of its penetration into our creaturely being. If God is merely impassible he has not made room for himself in our agonied existence, and if he is merely immutable he has neither time nor place for frail evanescent creatures in his unchanging existence. But the God who has revealed himself in Jesus as sharing our lot is the God who is free to make himself poor, that we through his poverty might be made rich, the God invariant in love but not impassible, constant in faithfulness but not immutable.'[4]

It is understandable that for this theology the integrity and the credibility of the Christian Gospel are at stake if God is not in his own eternal being what he is toward us in his incarnate activity in Jesus Christ, for then there would be no movement of God's own being in the life, passion, and resurrection of the Saviour of the world. But it is also understandable that, when the inherent unity of being and act in God forced upon theological understanding a conception of God in which movement belongs to his eternal being, this should initiate a revolution in the basic concept of being which removed it from the static conceptions that prevailed in Platonic, Aristotelian, Stoic, and Neoplatonic circles, which in turn opened up the way for a corresponding change in our understanding of created or contingent being which must also be construed on its own level not in a static but in a dynamic manner.[5]

How then are we to relate these basic theological ideas, set free from the encasement of dualist modes of thought in the ancient and mediaeval eras, to the world-view that derives from classical physics, and to the determinism that developed out of its conception of the mechanistic universe?

It was, of course, Newton who supplied the basic paradigms for this development, but those paradigms derive from his strangely ambiguous conception of the relation of God to the universe. For him the rationality and the stability of the universe were grounded in the ultimate rationality and stability of God its Creator and Preserver. However, on the one hand Newton's God is inertially attached to the universe in a grand synthesis which makes him through absolute time and space the supreme regulative principle by which the whole system of the world is held together, while on the other hand he is so transcendently related to the universe that he is deistically detached from it in his eternal impassibility and immutability. Through identifying absolute time with the eternal duration of God, and absolute space with the infinite presence of God, which together constitute the medium in which all things are contained, structured, and moved, Newton accounted for the natural and immutable order of the universe which operated through mechanical causes and with mathematical precision. Nevertheless, mechanical causes of that kind, Newton claimed, could not be extrapolated to account for the origin of the kind of order that obtains within the universe—for that a different kind of 'cause' is required, 'the agency of will'. Expressed differently this means that the laws of nature do not apply to those creative processes by which what is nature came into being, but only to those observable processes of a nature that is already in being. This is a point of considerable significance, for it means, in Newton's view, that the universe cannot be conceived to be a mechanical system complete and consistent in itself, for its immanent order is not completely explainable within that system, but the universe may be conceived as a consistent mechanism if it is related to 'the counsel' of a 'voluntary and intelligent Agent' beyond it, the living God who rules over all.[6]

However, in Newton's view, God is also required to fulfil certain functions within the immanent processes of the universe, both in respect of those features which appeared to him to defy mechanical law and with respect to certain 'irregularities' which he detected in the systematic motions of bodies in the solar and stellar systems. Unless God's power, he held, were constantly deployed to maintain balance and harmony, considerable disturbance would result.[7] That is to say, God is thought of as performing a *regulative* part within the systematic connections of bodies in motion in order to resolve certain irregularities and prevent others. Apparently, this looks like a rejection of complete determinism, that is, a view of the universe as a completely closed system of cause and effect; but actually it is a calling in of divine or final causes to make up for deficiencies in the chain of mechanical causes where divine causes are made to operate in connection with and on the same level as mechanical causes. Newton seems to have confounded the all-comprehending or containing rôle of God in creating the universe and conferring upon it an ordered rationality, and the rôle of God in regulating the chain of efficient causes, supplying deficiencies and coping with irregularities. This confusion had unfortunate consequences in the history of thought. The second rôle of God to the world in connection with the gaps opened in our scientific knowledge of the universe was inevitably ousted as soon as the alleged irregularities yielded to more thoroughgoing explanation in accordance with Newton's laws of motion. That is what happened, of course, with Laplace who claimed to be able to give a complete account of the universe according to self-regulating and eternal law, which removed alleged irregularities and deficiencies, so that there was no need for the 'hypothesis' 'God'.[8] By doing away with the rôle of God in regulating and harmonizing mechanical connections within the universe, Laplace imagined that he had demonstrated the internal stability of the universe as though it were complete and consistent in itself. But this has not proved to be the case; hence Newton's primary point remains: the impossibility of reducing the universe completely to a mechanical system, and therefore the need for some non-mechanical agency to be correlated with it as an intelligible whole and provide the sufficient reason for its accessibility to scientific investigation.[9] Thus the relation of the universe to God seems to be steadily forced on us by the advance of science itself. This has evidently proved to be the case as epistemological and cosmological dualisms which have so long prevailed in Western thought have yielded to the revolution associated with relativity theory, but in the era of Newton and his successors it was very difficult to appreciate in the context of causal determinism that arose out of the attempt to qualify all motion and subject the entire realm of nature to mechanical law, not least when the concept of a mechanistic universe hardened into an unquestioned dogma and dominated the whole range of science. Behind all that development, however, and fostering it, lay a contradiction in Newton's theology, between his concept of God as an inertial power, detached in his absoluteness, and his concept of God's rôle within the mechanistic or causal system of the world. The fall away of the latter left Western thought geared to a massive deism, in which God cannot be thought of as interacting with the universe he has made without interfering in its natural operations, which ruled out any idea of miracle as some unacceptable suspension of natural law. That this basic deism lay in Newton's own thought is clear from his vehement rejection of the teaching of Athanasius on the incarnation, and his acceptance of the views of Arius, on the ground that God could no more become incarnate in the universe which he himself inertially contained by the space and time which constituted his divine 'sensorium', than a pail could be contained by itself as part of its contents. From the point of view of theology, then, Newton's idea of the 'freedom' of God as an inertial absolute, carries with it the concept of a universe that is not free but imprisoned within its own systematic necessities. Far from the freedom of the universe being grounded in the transcendent freedom of God, the universe as a closed continuum of cause and effect is grounded in the inertial, impassible system that is called 'God'. The theological lesson to be learned here is that deism and determinism go together. From the point of view of natural science, what is at stake is the radical dualism between absolute time and space identified with the containing life and presence of God, and relative, apparent time and space of this world, together with the masterful container notion of time and space with which all this is construed.

Newton's great achievement lay in discovering with the aid

of 'fluxions' or differential equations (which he invented at the same time) the dynamic nature of the universe and reaching, as Einstein expressed it, a clear conception of 'differential law' appropriate to it.[10] This is not to be understood as if he read differential equations into nature, for they are no more than mathematical tools with which we seek to measure variation and change, and through which we seek to apprehend nature in its constancy and yet variability. However, Newton insisted on presenting the dynamic universe and interpreting continuous motion within the *idealized* framework of a geometry of relations between rigid bodies independent of time.[11] This had the effect of clamping down upon everything in the universe a hard deterministic or mechanical structure. If that idealized Euclidean framework is dismantled, then the universe is found to manifest itself, not as a closed deterministic system, but as a continuous and open system of contingent realities and events with an inherent unifying order. As such its internal consistency must finally depend on relation to an objective ground of rationality beyond the boundaries of the contingent universe itself. That is, as I understand it, the effect of Einstein's reconstruction of classical physics: a finite but unbounded universe with open, dynamic structures grounded in a depth of objectivity and intelligibility which commands and transcends our comprehension. Of course this does not mean that classical Newtonian physics is simply rejected: rather is it all the more firmly established on its own level as a limiting case of field physics, so that its cause and effect relations hold good only within the brackets of recognized abstractions, and as such have only a limited range of application. Such an outlook upon the universe and its immanent order is certainly far more congenial to classical theology of the Nicene type than that of ancient, mediaeval or classical physics operating with dualistic structures in their cosmologies and epistemologies.

At this point in order to open out the context for fresh theological construction it may be useful, from the position we have reached in scientific understanding of the universe today after its departure from the mechanical foundation of everything, to look at several lines of critical reaction to traditional mechanical determinism.

While all physical nature is determinate in the sense that its relations and conditions are open to mathematical calculation, mechanical determinism does not appear to be a feature inherent in nature itself.[12] Determinism arises where we develop a particulate or discontinuous view of nature without regard to continuous fields of force extended throughout space and time, and thus operate with an artificial abstraction of causal relations from cohesion or the force that holds particles together. This is evident from the very outset of classical physics when discrete particles, considered only as material points at an infinitesimal instant of time and regarded as connected only through their external relations, were held to act directly and instantaneously on one another irrespective of the distances between them. To be tenable such a view of particles in motion required an unchanging, stable, and uniform framework beyond the particles themselves to provide an invariable reference for their instantaneous position. That is what Newton supplied in his conception of absolute, unvarying space, empty of anything that might affect the configuration of events contained within it, and absolute in the sense that it remains unaffected by anything that happens within it, while inertially conditioning all particles in motion in the universe and constituting them into a comprehensive mechanical system. It is this stabilization of space, giving it uniformity and symmetry, within which causes operate, that gives them their deterministic character, a one-way necessitarian relation between cause and effect similar to the logical relation which obtains between the premises and the conclusion contained in the premises. Here we have the logico-causal structure which was taken as the ground for positivist notions of prediction.

Everything changes, however, when space is no longer regarded as empty but filled with matter and energy, and when time enters effectively into the equation as an inalienable ingredient in the intervening relations between particles or events affecting their configuration—that is, when all absolutes fall away, and space and time are no longer regarded as empty or unvarying containers but as relations intrinsic to the on-going contingent processes of the universe, so that particles or events are to be regarded as spatially and temporally extended and not as simply contained in space

and time. And the change is deeper still when the co
space-time is introduced, and thus the continuous, d
metrical field, with a reciprocal action between it a
constituent matter and energy of the universe, unifying and
ordering everything within it. While this did not resolve away
entirely the duality of particle and field it did eliminate the
damaging dualism inherent in Newtonian physics, replacing
its rigid absolutes in the foundations of science with a more
profoundly objective, unitary dynamic relatedness inherent
in the structure of the universe, invariant for any and every
observer, but which cannot be construed in terms of a closed
axiomatic framework.

It is sometimes argued that Einstein, in his critical handling
of the way quantum theory was developing, retreated back
into determinism whereas it is quantum theory that really
breaks free from it. It seems to me that if anything the
reverse may rather be the case, especially when we compare
relativity theory with quantum theory in its Copenhagen/
Göttingen form. Quantum theory thus formulated, on the
ground of the alleged impossibility of getting behind the
observer and his measuring instruments at the same time,
limited itself to offering an account of the physical realities of
nature only indirectly through statistical calculus of the probabilities of their occurrence or change in time, and thus makes
no claim to represent the field of their material and dynamic
structure. While Einstein himself contributed to such a statistical approach to quantum theory, he refused to be content
with it, for the basic function of science, as he regarded it, is
not to offer a statistical account of the acts of observation but
to lay bare the structures of reality as far as that is possible, as
had been done in relativity theory. In demanding this also of
quantum theory Einstein was not lapsing back into determinism but, as Pauli has shown in several letters to Max Born,
was being 'realistic', that is, attempting to reach a direct
description of reality.[13] To accuse Einstein of determinism
is to make the serious mistake of confusing his concept of
'field laws' with that of 'mechanical laws'. That would be
tantamount to interpreting his concept of invariance in field
laws in terms, not of relativistic, but of classical transform-
ations concerned with the identity of a substance as geometrically defined in respect of location in space and time, and

thus as an unchanging aspect of nature persisting through all apparent change.[14] The kind of intrinsic dynamic relatedness which Einstein was concerned to bring to light in quantum theory is quite different from that which obtains in the mechanical laws of classical physics. If anything it was contemporary quantum theory which appeared to be guilty of this, not only because a statistical approach leads in a deterministic direction, but because by operating with two distinct concepts of matter and field and by assuming that matter and energy are not continuously distributed through space, it appeared to be operating still within the frame of basic concepts taken over from classical mechanics. Certainly for a layman like myself it seems evident that it is only from within the framework of determinism that one can operate with ideas such as 'indeterminacy', while to put this down to our interference with the phenomena being investigated is really to argue that indeterminism has only to do with our limitations in observation and not with the objective connections in nature which remain deterministic. Actually, however, quantum theory even in the Copenhagen/Göttingen form does operate with events which cannot be construed in terms of classical mechanics and which spell the end of determinism, for example the behaviour of an electron sometimes as a particle and sometimes as a wave, the decaying of a particle at one moment and not at another, the emission of an electron in one direction rather than another, not to speak of the way in which, according to later theory, particles 'contain' or 'interpenetrate' one another, where clearly a new mode of thinking is required appropriate to a different kind of connection or order intrinsic to nature. Be that as it may, 'indeterminacy' appears to have objective ground in natural law.[15]

The most significant move away from determinism, however, is found in Einstein's development of the dynamic field of space-time, in which time itself enters with space into the structure of the field, for that has the effect of radically undermining the classical notion of matter, and therefore of material or physical explanation. Here we have a relativization of causality similar to the relativization of time, which deepens the concept of order in fundamental relationships, but leaves classical causality behind as an artificial adjustment of thought through split space and time to a lower and limited level of structural connections. The dropping of all absolutes in Newtonian or Kantian form which the classical notion of causality required, had the effect of liberating nature from the unwarranted imposition upon it of human abstractions so that it was allowed to disclose itself in its own natural or intrinsic order which is of an open, contingent kind, with variables which we are unable to tame by our idealized or mechanical patterns of thought. What Einstein sought to do, therefore, was to penetrate into the immanent intelligibilities of the continuous dynamic field of contingent events and bring them to appropriate formulation, but all this depends on a way of thinking which overcomes the duality of matter (or particle) and field, which Einstein himself was not able finally to achieve, although he kept on insisting that 'it is not the charges nor the particles but the field in the space between the charges and the particles which is essential for the description of physical phenomena'.[16]

If I understand recent developments in quantum field theory and particle theory correctly, this is the direction in which thought has been moving, that is, into a situation in which particles are conceived as four-dimensional entities in space-time, as concentrations of energy interconnected in fields of force, where many 'particles' are not so much particles as nodules of exchanging connection between strongly interacting particles, and where the fields of force themselves are as significant as the particles they hold together in a profound configuration of dynamic relations. Here where the distinction between particles and interconnecting forces diminishes we move even further away from classical mechanics and its deterministic conception of causal order obtaining between separated bodies in motion which retain their substantial identity through all changes in space and time. Here we have a relational type of order which is at once dynamic and open, which appears to require for its expression a differential calculus of possibility and consistency rather than of probability, for the nature of the universe as it discloses itself to us constantly takes us by surprise. A calculus of potentiality envisages something less than an open possibility, for it would foreclose possibility along the lines of actualities already grasped. It would be a calculus operating along the line of some latent entelechy, and therefore with a measure of predictability, instead of along a line continuously open to quite new and unpredictable variations deriving from the unlimited spontaneity of the universe. A calculus of potentiality would seem to operate with a form of the active reason (*intellectus agens*) through which we give shape to any possibility as a potentiality preformed by our understanding of actuality.

In the immediately preceding discussion we have had in view mainly the nature of the universe as it comes to light through our investigations in physics, and so have been concerned with the kind of order disclosed at different levels of physical reality. But what do we find when we move beyond these limits to investigate other aspects of the universe where other sciences are appropriate? Western thought has suffered here considerably from the Kantian idea that space and time are *a priori* forms of intuition, and that substance and causality are *a priori* categories of the understanding, which together constitute the frame which gives our knowledge of any possible empirical experience a universal and necessary form. That is to say, by transferring absolute space and time from the mind of God to the mind of the human knower, Kant generalized classical determinism to make it affect all that man can know. Relativity and quantum theory together demonstrate that this does not hold even for the content of all physical theories, but with the dethroning by Einstein of absolutes in the Newtonian or Kantian sense, there is certainly no justification for such an extrapolation of the kind of order we find through physics, let alone causal order, to other realms of human knowledge. Hence we must ask, What is the kind of order that the contingent universe in its multivariable nature reveals in other aspects of our experience of it, for example when we have to do with live realities or events? The contingent nature of these realities and events requires us to answer that question only out of the realities and events themselves, by penetrating into their own structures. On the other hand, it is an inalienable assumption of all scientific inquiry that the universe is everywhere immanently rational and as such open to rational apprehension, which would not be the case if there were conflicting rationalities or patterns of order embedded in it. We operate with the conviction, then, that there is one pervasive rational order throughout the universe, so that we do not believe we are really in touch with reality if we come up with results in one aspect of the universe which conflict with those we derive elsewhere. But this does not rule out the fact that the order inherent in the universe is manifold in character, and that there are different modes of rational order which while remaining distinctive nevertheless do not conflict but contribute to the multivariable character of the whole.

This indeed is what appears to be the case, for there are at least four basic modes of rational order with which we have to do, and to which we may refer in terms of *number, logos, organic* or *organismic form*, and *aesthetic form*. They are all distinctive forms of rational order which demand distinctive expression, but far from conflicting with one another they all appear to involve each other, although in different ways. It is sometimes the case that when we operate with an unusual combination of two or more of them in some inquiry, we discover new elements in nature which would otherwise have eluded us. This makes us feel that to pursue only one mode of order on its own in an exclusive way is an artificial abstraction which nature punishes by limiting our discoveries through it. This is certainly what has often happened when we acted as though the kind of order amenable to number, i.e. to quantifying operations leading to mathematically formulable laws, is the only order acceptable to rigorous science. From this point of view the electromagnetic field must be a 'miracle' to classical mechanics, while living organisms are more of a 'miracle', for they are not open to treatment even through partial differential equations. This is also the case when again and again we insist that the kind of orderly connection in thought which we have developed from analysis of language, in logic, especially when it is bound up with the subject-predicate structure of Western language, is the only acceptable form within which to give rational expression to the kinds of connection we lay bare in nature. For example in quantum theory we evidently have to do with a connection which is not amenable to that kind of logical treatment, but one which requires a new kind of material logic (*Sachlogik*) appropriate to it. In any case we have to be aware of confounding temporal connection with logical connection, for in the dynamic space-time continuum, as indeed in all motion, we operate with the principle of sufficient reason and not with the principle of non-contradiction which is concerned with necessary relations.

Biological science is particularly instructive here. We have considerable difficulty in laying bare and in representing the inner order of the organic field without converting it into numerate order.

This seems to be due to our failure to develop the appropriate language with which to express organismic form, for without such an appropriate language we are unable to grasp and develop anything like the *biologic* which we need with which to bring to rational formulation the dynamic laws of living organisms. That is to say, in the field of biological inquiry (where we are concerned with matter-energy-life) we need to operate with some apposite mental instrument, similar to the way we operate with the differential calculus or four-dimensional geometry in physics, to enable us to isolate and understand distinctively organismic connections— otherwise we are tempted to lapse into some sort of determinism through the imposition upon the subject-matter of an unwarranted form of quantification, or into a reductionist mode of thought in which we allow the distinctive organismic form to slip through the net of our inquiries.

Without discussing this further, let us pick out several points which are relevant for our theme.

1. With living organisms we have to do with morphological structures which resist attempts to formulate their intrinsic order in terms of cause and effect. Here we certainly have a unifying order of a remarkable kind, but it is not amenable to mechanical explanation, or to mechanical explanation only.

2. Even if we were to apply the cause-effect relation to the living activity of organisms, we would not be able to interpret the 'effect' merely by reference to an antecedent 'cause', for the new state that emerges cannot be accounted for by a rearrangement of previous states, since quite new elements are involved which cannot be traced back to the causal conditioning of previous states. Here there takes place a creative development of a previous state, which takes up

the old into the new in a transformed way, so that if we are to bring laws of living organic activity to formulation we will have to operate with some sort of organismic transformation which might bear a relation to the order entailed at a lower level, parallel to the relation between relativistic transformation and classical transformation in physics. That is to say, we have to reckon here with a basic change in order from that which obtains at the physico-chemical level, and certainly a non-deterministic order which is multivariable and open in accordance with the contingent motion of live realities and events.

3. We would have to reckon with the fact that organismic order of this kind does not conflict with but reposes upon the lower order of physico-chemical structure such as we have in the DNA molecule, while nevertheless it transcends explication merely in terms of that 'lower order'. This seems to me to indicate that we need something like but beyond the second law of thermodynamics for the formulation of organismic order, but, unlike the classical formulation of the second law which holds within a closed system, this would have to hold with open, non-equilibrium systems in the whole range of biological transformation and evolution.

Be that as it may, here we are up against basic issues which have already arisen in our discussion: the requirement to take contingence seriously in its own right as contingence, and not as some form of concealed necessity, and the impossibility of a rational system being both complete and consistent at the same time. Newton failed to take contingence seriously and thus contributed to the Western tradition of determinism, but he did appreciate the fact that the system of the world could not be based finally on itself or be explained out of itself in terms of its own immanent order, but required reference to a different concept of order beyond it. Leibniz tried to take contingence seriously, and in so doing formulated the principle of sufficient reason to replace the principle of non-contradiction in understanding motion, but he seems to have let in a form of determinism by the back door through his principle of 'maximum determination' in the divine reason for the creation, and possibly also in his idea of 'pre-established harmony', which prevented him from going the length of Newton in appreciating the incompleteness of the created universe as a consistent system.[17] It is, I believe, in the realm of biology that we can discern the importance of these issues more readily than in physics. Here we have to do with living realities which by their very nature have an independence and power to disclose themselves to us in an indefinite range of unexpected manifestations. And here we find an ontological stratification in the universe comprising a sequence of rising levels, each higher one controlling the boundaries of the one below it and embodying thereby the joint meaning of the particulars situated on the lower level, which implies, in Michael Polanyi's words, 'that all meaning lies in the higher levels of reality that are not reducible to the laws by which the ultimate particulars of the universe are controlled.'[18] Together all this tells us that the universe in its immanent structure comprises a hierarchy of levels of reality which are open upward but not reducible downward, for no one level provides the sufficient reason for its own contingent order which may be formalized only through reference to another level or to other levels beyond it. The same principle, of course, applies to the universe as a whole, which is thus to be regarded as an essentially open system for precisely as an intelligible whole it requires a sufficient reason beyond itself. That is to say, the universe confronts us as an open, heterogeneous contingent system characterized throughout by coordinated strata of natural coherences of orderly connections of different kinds in and through which we discover an uncircumscribed range of rationality grounded beyond the universe itself but reaching so far beyond us that with all our science we realize we may apprehend it only at its comparatively elementary levels. That is the universe to which we ourselves belong, with the structure of which we share in the distinctive structure of our own human being, so that we find our own rationality intimately connected with its rationality and as open to what is beyond us as the universe itself to the ultimate source and ground of all that is in the unlimited reality and rationality of the Creator. Indeed it is man himself with his inquiring rationality who constitutes in the structure of the space-time universe the boundary point where it is open beyond itself, and where the mystery of its meaning becomes disclosed, insofar as he allows his mind to fall under the power of revelation from beyond.

It is with such an understanding of the universe and its immanent order that the basic ideas of classical Christian theology as to the relation between God and the universe are emancipated, as it were, from the constrictions of a dualist outlook in which a God of inertial motion and a determinate universe governed by necessary relations are correlated with each other. From the point of view of Christian theology, in its creation out of nothing the universe has had conferred freely upon it a created rationality of its own derived from (not participating in) the uncreated rationality of God, yet transcendentally (not ontologistically) grounded in it. Likewise, in its creation out of nothing the universe is given a freedom of its own derived from (but not as an extension of) the self-sufficient freedom of God, yet transcendentally (mediately, not immediately) grounded in it. Further, since the universe is not only created out of nothing but maintained in its creaturely being through the constant interaction of God with it, who will not let it slip away from him into nothing but grounds its existence on his eternal faithfulness, the universe is given a stability beyond anything of which it is capable in its own contingent state. It is this combination of contingence, rationality, freedom and stability of the universe, under God, which gives it its remarkable character, and which makes scientific exploration of the universe not only possible for us but incumbent upon us.

On the other hand, while the universe is maintained in this way through the continuous interaction of God with it, that interaction rests upon the free ground of God's own transcendent being and rationality such that far from there being a necessary relation between God and the universe and the universe and God, God remains utterly free and is not at the disposal of the conceptions and necessities of any deductive argumentation or logical compulsion on our part. This is not to say that God is only arbitrarily related to the universe by the mere fiat of his omnipotent will and power, but rather that he makes his own eternal truth the creative source and determinant ground of the contingent order of the universe, in such a way that while he is in no way indebted to the universe, the universe is altogether indebted to him for what it is. As it was created out of nothing the universe might have been quite different from what it is, but now that it has come into being, and in the way that it has, it is possessed of a contingent rationality bound up with what it is as it came from God, and thus has also a contingent 'necessity' of its own, in the sense that it cannot not be what it now is as this universe possessed of this and not some other created rationality.

Two points emerge from this which need further elucidation.

1. Regarded in itself the universe is what it is, this one and only universe which has come into being, but considered from the side of God's free creation it is only one of all possible universes since it might have been very different. This means that we must think of God's relation to the universe in terms of an infinite variability bound up with his unlimited freedom and rationality. As such God remains the free creative ground of the universe even though by bringing it into existence he has actualized one possibility among all the others which has the effect of ruling out the others as really impossible or at least unentertainable. This is the only kind of 'necessity' that the universe has, that it cannot now be other than it is. But since this 'necessity' is freely grounded in the infinite freedom and rationality of God who remains variationally related to what he has made, it is the kind of 'necessity' that is entirely consistent with the freedom of contingent reality. Far from allowing us to understand the immanent rationality of the universe thus brought into being in necessitarian or deterministic terms, it obliges us to take contingent freedom and contingent rationality with the utmost seriousness. It is because this freedom and rationality within the universe are contingent upon the infinite freedom and inexhaustible rationality of God that the universe meets our inquiries with an indefinite capacity for disclosing itself to us in ways which we could not suspect, manifesting structures or patterns which we are quite unable to anticipate *a priori*. Looked at from this point of view, determinism and the kind of predictability associated with it arise from a false process of thought in which we read the end result of a contingent happening back along the line of its movement into its beginning as though it had to take this course from the very start, thus mistakenly converting

contingent 'necessity' into some kind of logico-causal necessity. Moreover, this has the unfortunate effect of converting structural field laws which arise in an *a posteriori* manner into *a priori* principles enabling us to argue deductively and prescriptively beyond what is empirically and contingently given, that is beyond the contingent structures of which natural laws are *post hoc* formulations. Certainly the rejection of this backward way of reading open contingent events into the conditioning pattern of antecedent causes, reversing the movement of their happening, falls into line with the theological understanding of the freedom of the universe as grounded in the freedom of God, and of the open character and endless spontaneity and surprise of its natural order which is ultimately explicable only from beyond itself in the infinite differentiality of divine rationality and its inexhaustible source of possibility.[19]

2. This conception of an infinite differential in the rationality of God allows us to express the transcendent freedom of God from any alleged necessity, spatio-temporal, causal, or logical, in his relationship with the universe he has created, without making him arbitrary or inscrutable. On the other hand, since the universe has had conferred upon it in and through its creation a contingent rationality of its own, which embodies what we have called a 'contingent necessity', that is, its impossibility, now that it has come into being, of being other than it is in relation to the eternal rationality of God, its on-going processes are characterized by intrinsic structures which God himself, not only by creating the universe but by maintaining it in being, affirms as real even for himself in the actuality of his relation to the universe, and which therefore he obliges us to respect as upheld by his divine sanction. This applies to the orderly objective connections which we bring to light through our scientific inquiries and seek to formulate as 'laws of nature', but since they are what they objectively are in the creation through its relation to the Creator himself, we cannot think of his interaction with the universe as in any way interfering with its laws or thereby introducing disorder into what he has made, but rather the reverse, as reinforcing its contingent rationality and giving constancy to its immanent order.

It is in that light also that we must regard the incarnation

of the Son of God who as the eternal Logos is the divine
agent of creation through whom it derives its rational order.
Hence the incarnation is not to be regarded as an intrusion
into the creation or into the structures of space and time,
but rather as the freely chosen way of God's rational love
in the fulfilment of his eternal purpose for the universe.
Through astonishing self-communication to the creature he
has established in the incarnation a supreme axis, as it were,
for direct interaction with the creation within its contingent
existence and structure, which is at the same time the pledge
of his eternal faithfulness that he will never let go what he
has made, allowing it to decay and crumble away into nothingness, but will uphold and redeem it and consummate through
it the purpose of his rational love. All this applies directly to
the activity of the incarnate Son of God in the human life
which he has come to share with us, for it is a direct extend-
ing of the operations of God into the life and destiny of
human being within the contingent structures of space and
time where, somehow, man is menaced by evil and his labile
existence is threatened with disorder and disintegration. It
is thus that we are to think of the miraculous acts of Jesus
within the limits, conditions, and objectivities of our world,
not as involving in any way the suspension of the space-time
structures which we call 'natural law', far less implying the
abrogation of the God-given order in nature they express,
but rather as the re-creating and deepening of that order in
the face of all that threatens to break it down through sin,
disease, violence, death, or evil of any kind. He overcomes
our disorder by bringing his own creative being redemptively
to bear upon our existence from within it, and deepens its
ordering by correlating it on its own contingent levels in a
new way with the power of his own transcendent life and
rationality, where its ultimate and sufficient reason is lodged.
Just as within the multi-levelled structures of the universe, as
they come to view through our scientific inquiries, we find
that each level of reality is finally integrated not through its
own operational connections but through relation to connections at a higher level, to which it is open at its own
'boundary conditions', so the incarnation as a whole provides,
as it were, the intersecting vertical dimension which gives the
horizontal coordinates of the universe the integrative factor

providing them with consistent and ultimate meaning, in a way which a merely deistic asymptotic relation between God and the universe could never do. Thus there are, it would seem, sets of circumstances or events in the life of Jesus, as he is presented in the Gospels, which do not seem to make sense to us when we regard them merely on the level of observable phenomena, for they conflict with the orderly way we are accustomed to interpret phenomena, but when we consider them in correlation with additional factors introduced from a higher level, they are discerned to present a profoundly intelligible pattern compelling the assent of our minds. That happens only in the framework created by the bearing of the incarnation upon the creation which provides the Gospel with its infinite dimension of depth grounded in the transcendent rationality of God. And that is precisely how the basic ideas of the relation of God to the universe arose in the Early Church which have had such a profound effect upon subsequent science and theology.

God and the Contingent Universe

The basic problem that faces us in the relations between theological science and natural science has to do with a deep paradox in the heart of natural science itself. The understanding of the contingent nature of the cosmos upon which all empirico-theoretical inquiry rests, derives not from natural science but from Judaeo-Christian theology, i.e. from the doctrine of God as Creator of the orderly universe, who brought it into existence out of nothing and who continuously preserves it from lapsing back into chaos and nothingness. Nevertheless scientific investigation of this created order, rigorously in accordance with its distinctive nature, must be pursued without reference to God or any recourse to theological reasoning. The paradox may be succinctly formulated in terms of two classical statements of Reformed theology: nothing can be established about contingence except through divine revelation (*nihil constat de contingentia nisi ex revelatione*), and, divine creation requires us to investigate the contingent world out of its own natural processes alone, without including God in the given (*acsi deus non daretur*).

Natural science tacitly assumes the contingence, as well as the orderliness, of the universe. If there were no order immanent in the universe, if there were chaos and not a cosmos, the universe would not be accessible to scientific knowledge; if the universe were not characterized by contingence, the laws of nature would be derived from it immediately and necessarily through logico-deductive processes without experimental questioning of nature to induce it to yield its secrets—which would make empirical science quite pointless.[1] It is through relying on the indissoluble bond between contingence and order in the universe that natural science has come to operate with the distinctive interconnection between experiment and theory which has characterized our greatest advances in knowledge of the physical world. Yet we cannot prove that there is order in the universe, for we have to assume it in order even to attempt proof of it;[2] while genuine contingence is something that natural science on its own cannot come up with, but is rather something that natural science, through its ways of determining regularities in nature and formulating universal laws, is always on the point of resolving away.[3] Quite evidently science must assume conceptions and principles that are themselves not logically derivable, explainable, or provable, but without which it could not function.[4] Contingence and order are assumptions of that kind, yet we do not derive them from natural science but from a fundamental outlook upon the nature of the universe that is the correlative of a distinctive doctrine of God as the Creator of the universe.

Let it be granted from the standpoint of natural science that the conception of creation out of nothing is incomprehensible to us, because when we think about the creation of the universe by God we pass beyond the possibilities of our intramundane knowledge. It is basically the same difficulty that we meet in the derivative notion of contingence. Our scientific thought moves within the space-time domain of our empirical world and is confined within its immanent possibilities. Within this framework, contingence, if it is not inconceivable, at least cannot adequately be conceptually represented, and thus confronts us rather like a surd as something which is finally intractable to scientific formalization.[5] In the prosecution of our scientific inquiries we can only move along the intelligible relations and their sequences latent in the world until we reach the boundaries where they break off, and where we find it scientifically illegitimate to extend intramundane connections and possibilities beyond our actual world. This is particularly evident in cosmological inquiries, as we shall see later, where relentless research carries us to zero points before which physical laws, as we have formulated them, become critical and peculiar, and even predict their own downfall, as it were.[6] But that by no means puts a question to their intelligibility or validity, although it may require their revision as limiting cases of deeper and wider conceptions—yet that cannot go on *ad infinitum*, not if we are to be rigorously faithful to the contingence of the world. Our theories have come up against the limits set for us by the initial conditions of nature which, though they cannot be accounted for within the frame of our physical laws, are nevertheless essential to the rational enterprise of science.[7] We have pushed back our explanations to the ultimate assumptions on which they rested, and there becomes starkly disclosed the sheer contingence of the cosmos, although as such it is not demonstrable. But now we are forced to treat contingence not merely as a presupposition, but as an essential factor in scientific understanding and interpretation of the natural order. That is to say, contingence must take its place among the ultimate normative beliefs with which science operates, along with order, rationality, simplicity, etc.

That would seem to be the position which we have reached today, when the relation between science and contingence can no longer be kept at the tacit level. Throughout the universe, as we increasingly realize, contingent states of affairs are contingently related to other contingent states of affairs. Hence we cannot but give contingence an integral place in our fundamental data, and recognize that contingence characterizes the basic connections in nature which we seek to formulate in natural law. That is to say, contingence must be integrated into the basic structure of our scientific theories and explanations which means that physical laws themselves must be recognized as contingent. We shall return to this point.

This status of contingence in scientific theory and physical law has far-reaching implications which cannot be followed through to the end within the framework of natural science, for they carry our thought beyond it, as we are forced to make unverifiable judgements about unique events which we cannot relate to known examples, and about the ultimate singularity of our one and only universe itself. Since these implications are grounded in the intelligibility of the universe disclosed through our inquiries, they have the effect of opening doors onto the ultimate intelligible ground on which the universe and our knowledge of it finally rest. That meta-scientific reference of our thought cannot be avoided if the intelligibility of the universe is to be sustained in our belief— otherwise we would be cornered into a position which implied the utter pointlessness of the universe; and that would have the effect of putting a damning question mark against the whole rational enterprise of science. What happens, however, is something rather different. In the operations of our empirico-theoretical science, which presuppose and materially entail the contingence of the universe, we find ourselves grasped by its inherent relations in such a way as to be caught up in a reference of those relations beyond themselves. This is something we are familiar with in the structure of our scientific formulations, e.g. of some natural law, which we believe to hold good beyond the range of our empirical evidence for it, so that we are found committed to assertions about things we have as yet had no experience of.[8] We have a signal instance of this in the theory of relativity.[9] The intelligibility of the contingent world as a whole, within which the full import of our scientific connections is revealed, becomes progressively disclosed to us as locked into a dimension of intelligibility that transcends its manifestations in the patterns of the observable universe or our power to master it and reduce it to conceptual form. We find ourselves grasped by a commanding rationality, calling for our respect and obliging our assent to it beyond the range of our experience in the empirical world, a rationality of a higher order which makes semantic sense of the contingent universe and our commitment to explore and understand it. Correspondingly a correlative movement of thought is generated in us as the baffling interconnection of contingence and intelligibility in the universe cries out for an originating reason for this state of affairs. Thus the contingence and order, which our science presupposes and which it cannot account for within the frame of its own conceptual systems, carry us back to their ground in God the Creator. Much will depend, however, on how we understand contingence, and whether contingent intelligibility enters constructively into the basic concepts and principles on which our scientific theorizing rests in its 'hope of grasping the real in all its depth', as Einstein expressed it.[10]

In view of this we must take a closer look at the idea of contingence as it derives from Christian theology, and examine in some detail the reactions of natural science to it.

It may be helpful first to recall that the idea of contingence — as chance event or accident — was not altogether lacking in Greek thought, but there it was regarded as the polar antithesis to what is rational, the logically and causally necessary. Since the rational and the necessary were identified, the contingent could only be a synonym for what is irrational or unintelligible. Behind this lay two far-reaching presuppositions, affecting the ancient attitude to nature and science. First, a necessary and timeless relation between the world and God. This implied that the world was not created by God but was made the embodiment of divine reasons, the eternal forms which are the ground of its intelligibility. The effect of this was to make it virtually impossible to distinguish nature from God. Secondly, a radical dualism between the intelligible and the sensible, or form and matter. While the actual world was recognized as composed of form and matter, form was held to be the intelligible element, the definable timeless essence of things which makes them what they really are, but matter was held to be no more than the sensible element which is only accidentally related to the necessary, as appearance to reality or shadow to truth. Thus the sensible world was regarded as playing no more than a symbolic or illustrative role that is left behind as soon as we have to do with the rational and the real. This had the effect of restricting scientific knowledge to the realm of intelligible forms and changeless essences, and of reducing contingence simply to what is deficient in existence and lacking in rationality. The fact is, all Greek thought imprisoned the real world in an eternal system of rigid geometrical relations which determines the essence of all natural objects within it, so that knowledge of them is to be reached by way of rational deduction from their essences. Even if, as Aristotelians held, intelligible forms are immanent in the material or sensible world, making sense experience an inescapable condition of knowledge, the task of science is to effect a passage from the sensible to the intelligible, by abstracting the forms from the accidents of their embodiment in matter, and grounding knowledge only upon logically conceived causes that are necessarily and timelessly true. Since there is no necessity in accidental or contingent things, they are not open to logical or causal demonstration and cannot therefore provide evidential grounds for scientific knowledge. Thus contingence is entirely excluded from the basis and the content of science.

It is sometimes claimed that the Greek Atomists sought to make room for contingence when they deployed chance as well as necessity in their attempt at a unified theory of motion in the universe, that allowed for an infinite variety of random events. But chance thus conceived as a momentary fluctuation has an in-built tie to necessity as its logical correlate, and is in the end only a form of its manifestation. Chance or random events inevitably yield necessary patterns, for behind all chance there is ineluctable necessity. It is thus the task of science to disclose that necessity in all that takes place in the cosmos and so to establish throughout it self-regulating universal law, without any reference to anything else beyond—the cosmos is completely closed within its immanent necessary order. This implies the most complete rejection of any notion of creation. As Democritus expressed it, 'Nothing is created out of nothing.'[11] As in the rest of Greek thought, the assumed identity of rationality and necessity prevented contingence from being taken seriously in any way as a rational concept. Greek science could only think contingence up to a point, by thinking the element of necessity behind it, but that is to think contingence away, and indeed to deny it any possible place within rational cognitive activity. This accounts for the lack of the all-important empirical factor in ancient natural science, for the contingent and the empirical belong inseparably together. If nature is impregnated throughout by a necessary order, its regularities and laws can be discovered by pure *a priori* thought alone.[12]

Looking back it seems clear that a proper notion of contingence could not arise so long as there remained intact the determining presuppositions of Greek science, a necessary relation between the world and God, and the bifurcation between matter and form. A basic change in the attitude to nature and to science would have to take place, involving belief in the full reality of matter and the rationality of the contingent. But that required a profound change in the conception of God and his relation to the world, in fact, a radical doctrine of creation in which matter and form are regarded as equally created out of nothing and as inseparably unified in one pervasive contingent rational order in the universe. A divine creation of matter out of nothing would quire it to be treated as contingent reality, and not as unreal; and a divine creation of form out of nothing would require it to be differentiated from God's eternal and un-created rationality as contingent rationality. That is precisely the revolution that Judaeo-Christian theology injected into the foundations of Greek thought, while at the same time taking up its mathematical approach to the interpretation of nature as endowed by creation with a contingent rational order. The sheer novelty of the idea of creation out of nothing ran into an hostile reception which lingered on right up to the Reformation, for if an absolute beginning, coming into being out of nothing, was unthinkable, coming into being of intelligible form was even more unthinkable, for within the framework of Greek thought it could only mean that God, from whom all intelligible form and reality necess-arily and timelessly emanate, was himself created out of nothing—an idea which was, understandably, denounced as 'impious' and 'atheistic'.[13] Nevertheless, with the establish-ment of the Christian Church and its theology within the Graeco-Roman world, a revolutionary reconstruction of the fundamental framework of Greek thought set in, and the essential basis was laid for the development of empirico-theoretical science as we now know it.

The doctrine of the creation of the world out of nothing, of course, had its roots in the Old Testament and the Jewish understanding of the one God, who is the source of all that is outside himself, and who remains transcendent Lord over all that he has made, so that if he were to withdraw his creative and upholding presence from the creation it would lapse back into chaos and sheer nothingness. This teaching carried with it both a conception of the free (non-necessary) relation of God to the world, by which its contingent nature is constituted, and a unitary outlook upon the world creatively regulated by God's Word, which called in question all forms of religious, cosmological, and epistemological dualism. The creative act which brought the universe into being and form was not regarded as limited to its initial impulse, but as remaining unceasingly operative, preserving, unifying, and regulating all created existence which conversely was contingent in every respect of its nature and in no sense divine. Thus Judaism contributed to a profound understanding, not only of the absolute beginning, but of the continuity, stability, and uniformity of the natural world as grounded beyond itself in the constancy, faithfulness and reliability of God its Creator and Preserver.

However, it was Christian theology which radicalized and deepened the notion of contingence and gave reality to the notion of contingent intelligibility, through thinking out, in critical and constructive discussion with Greek science, the relation of the creation to the incarnation of God's Word in Jesus Christ within the spatio-temporal realities and intelligibilities of contingent existence in this world. The incarnation made it clear that the physical world, far from being alien or foreign to God, was affirmed by God as real even for himself. The submission of the incarnate Son of God to its creaturely limits, conditions, and objectivities, carried with it an obligation to respect the empirical world in an hitherto undreamed-of measure.

On the one hand, clear differentiation between the incarnation as the personal embodiment of God's Logos in a particular creaturely being, and the creation of the world out of nothing as an orderly cosmos, without the Logos being embodied in it, shattered the Greek idea that the intelligible order of the world is to be understood as a general embodiment of the divine Logos immanently within it, i.e. as its necessary, inner cosmological principle. That was to have very far-reaching effects in liberating the world from its inward bondage to divine changelessness, in virtue of which it was held to be impregnated with final causes, and thus in liberating nature from the iron grip of sheer necessity that resulted from them. On the other hand, the interrelation between the incarnation of the Logos and the creation of all things visible and invisible out of nothing by that same Logos, called for a profound rethinking of the relation between God and the world as one in which it is recognized that the radical distinction between uncreated and created being, between the uncreated rationality of God and the created rationality of the world, far from reducing the being and rationality of the contingent world to unreality and insignificance, establishes their reality and secures their significance, not in spite of, but precisely in their contingent character. That is to say, the incarnation has the constant effect of affirming the contingent intelligibility of the creation, reinforcing the requirement to accept it as the specific kind of rationality proper to the physical world, and as the only kind capable of providing evidential grounds for knowledge of the universe in its own natural processes.

The constitutive relation between God and the world which all this implies may be described as neither necessary nor arbitrary, but as both free and rational. The world needs God to be what it is, but God does not need the world to be what he is, the eternally self-existent God who is not dependent on anything other than himself. There is thus an asymmetrical relation between God and the world, characterized by perfect freedom on God's part and sheer dependence on the world's part. Since the Creator was free not to create, his act of creation is to be understood as an act of pure liberality and grace, i.e. a contingent act unconditioned by any necessity in God. It is because the created world is not necessary for God's being but is freely given by him a reality of its own distinct from his, that it is contingent, independent of any necessity in God but dependent upon the act of his beneficent will.

This contingent relation between God and the world is also irreversible, in the sense that while the world is continuously upheld in its being and form by the creative presence of God, there is no statically continuous and logically compelling relation between the being of the creature and the being of the self-existent Creator. Since there is no logical bridge between God and the world, there is no logical reversibility between them. If there were such a relation, knowledge of the created world and knowledge of God would be clamped together in such a way that we would derive knowledge of God necessarily and coercively from knowledge of the world, while knowledge of the world even in its natural operations would not be possible without constantly including God among the data. That would mean lapsing back into the old Greek view that the rational forms of the Deity are immanently and materially embodied in the universe, which, as we saw, eliminates the conditions necessary for the emergence of empirical science.

To reject that view is not to hold that the relation between God and the world is merely arbitrary, but quite the reverse.

It is to operate with a relation between the underived, creative rationality of God and the derived, created rationality of the world. Far from isolating the world from God, this contingent relation between them means that the world even in its creaturely otherness from God, is held continuously in such an ontological relation to God, the source of all rational order, that there is creatively imparted to it a rationality of its own which is not incongruous with God's rationality. What we cannot understand is that God who has no need of the world should have reason to create such a rational world, yet it is that reason hidden deep in God that ultimately lies behind all the reasonableness of the created order. In so far as that reason is disclosed in the incarnation, it is to be equated with the sheer mystery of God's love which knows no reason beyond its own ultimateness as the love that God is. That is to say, the reason for the creation is theologically traced back to the free, ungrudging will of God's love to create a reality other than himself which he correlates so closely with himself that it is made to reflect and shadow forth on its contingent level his own inner rationality and order. That is the ultimate ground for what Einstein called the 'incomprehensible comprehensibility' of the universe which evoked from him as a man of science constant wonder and deep sense of religious awe. It was with reference to this that he sometimes appealed to the Leibnizian notion of 'preestablished harmony' behind the 'miracle' of *Verständlichkeit*.

The conceptions of contingence and contingent intelligibility that derive from the Christian doctrine of creation are not easy to represent in precise conceptual terms because of the asymmetrical and irreversible relation between God and the world we have just been discussing. What makes contingence so baffling is the peculiar interlocking of dependence and independence that it involves. The independence of the world depends entirely upon the free creative act of God to give it being and form wholly differentiated from himself, but that is then an independence that is delimited by the dependence that anchors the world beyond itself in the freedom of the Creator. More concretely, this means that in creating the world God gave it a natural condition and status of its own in such a way that in order to do it justice we are obliged to concentrate on it for its own sake. Thus while on the one hand we cannot investigate the contingent world scientifically out of its own contingent processes without, as it were, a methodological turning away from knowledge of God, on the other hand, we cannot adequately apprehend the radical nature of contingence except from the perspective of the Creator and his free act of creation. Hence the point of the theological statement: *nihil constat de contingentia nisi ex revelatione*. The mystery of contingence cannot be grasped or thought out within the framework of the latent processes of the contingent world or their inherent lawfulness: its deepest secret lies outside its own reality.

There is no intrinsic reason in the universe why it should exist at all, or why it should be what it actually is: hence we deceive ourselves if in our natural science we think that we can establish that the universe could only be what it is.[14] The universe is not some sort of *perpetuum mobile*, a self-existing, self-supporting, self-explaining magnitude, wholly consistent and complete in itself and thus imprisoned within a pointless circularity of inescapable necessities. On the contrary, the universe constitutes an essentially *open* system with an ontological and intelligible reference beyond its own limits which cuts the circuit of any possible closure of its internal processes re-entrantly upon themselves, and thereby gives them their distinctive intelligibility. Thus it belongs to the very nature of the universe that the consistency of its own independent status and condition is incomplete and requires to be completed beyond itself. That is another way of saying that the independence of the universe is both grounded in and limited by its radical dependence. Given that dependence, openness, or reference of the universe beyond itself which is part of what contingence means, contingence also represents the fact—so important for natural science—that the universe is endowed with an autonomous character both as a whole and throughout its immanent relations, with features and patterns and operational principles which belong to it as by intrinsic natural right, and which require an autonomous mode of investigation appropriate to their distinctive nature and integrity. That is why contingence must be assiduously respected, and must not be rationalized away as some unfortunate element of deficiency

or inexplicability in nature from which science must abstract
in order to give a consistent, rational account of the universe.
Rather is contingence to be regarded as a basic and essential
feature of the universe, a constituting condition of its reality
and actuality.

This applies particularly to the nature of the intelligibility
of the contingent universe. Here theology operates with a
basic relation between the uncreated but creative rationality
of God and the created rationality of the world which
corresponds to it and reflects it in the modes of contingent
existence. The transcendent relation that obtains between
God and the creation led Christian thought to replace the
Greek idea of substantial forms or changeless essences with
that of intelligible *laws* expressing the kind of order proper
to objective contingency. This entailed a very different
conception of law from that of the prevailing immanentist
tradition in Graeco-Latin thought, in accordance with which
natural law, bound up with belief in the divinity of the
cosmos, was held to be a determinate manifestation of the
immutable, eternal, divine Logos indwelling and regulating
the cosmos. Such an equation of natural law with the immanent necessity of the divine reason implied a total rejection
of anything like contingent objectivity or intelligibility.

The Christian conception of law relates to the legislative
activity of the transcendent God, who does not embody his
own eternal Logos in nature as its universal law, but who
through the unifying and rationalizing power of his Logos
creatively imparts to the world as he creates it a pervasive
rational order on its own level subordinate to himself on his
transcendent level, as its determinant ground. The creation
of the universe as an autonomous reality distinct from God
while dependent on him also involves the endowment of the
universe with autonomous structures of its own. Natural law,
thus understood, refers to the God-given normative patterns
in the universe and has to do with the intrinsic truth or
objective intelligibility of contingent being.

The distinctive relation between the contingent intelligibility of the universe and God may be described in various
ways. The biblical tradition preferred to speak of it in terms
of the creative address of God's Word which summons
the processes of the contingent world into orderly and

harmonious antiphonal response. Thus there is generated throughout the universe under the creative power of God's Word a creaturely correspondence, a contingent language, answering obediently to the voice of the Creator. In this perspective natural science may well be regarded as the experimental questioning of nature in which we seek to induce it to tell us about itself in terms of its own natural language. Early Christian theology sought to give an account of contingent rationality in terms of space and time which are the bearers of all rational order within the universe, but which were brought into being out of nothing along with the universe as features of its contingent processes or relational patterns of its natural operations. We ourselves as rational beings came into existence within this universe of space and time and as such are bound to space and time as modes of the rational order which we share. But God is not spatially or temporally bound to the universe, for he is transcendentally free and sovereign over the whole created order as its Creator and Lawgiver. In this context, laws of nature are not immanent divine necessities but empirical sequences and regularities, invariant relations, which God has imparted to nature amidst all the changes and varieties of its contingent processes. Laws of nature in this sense have to do with real connections in nature: they are not abstract generalizations, idealized laws prescinded from concrete, empirical reality, but objective contingent consistencies.

Regarded in themselves, natural laws as laws of contingent reality have a limited validity, for, while they are economic descriptions of autonomous normative structures in the universe, they are what they ultimately are as *laws* by reference to the commanding and unifying rationality of God the Creator and Sustainer of the universe. Thus from a theological perspective the underlying connection, the ultimate consistency, in natural laws is grounded beyond their limits in God's creative upholding of the contingent universe by which he links it to his own rationality, constancy, and reliability as its transcendent ground. But for that very reason the universe is characterized throughout not by a static but by a dynamic stability, not by closed rigid structures but by open-ordered structures, not by necessary truths of reason but by contingent truths which defy complete mathematical formalization.

A further cognate aspect of contingence and contingent intelligibility, which we have already had occasion to note,[15] must be brought back into the discussion at this point, before we go on to consider the reactions of natural science. This has to do with the astonishing flexibility and multivariability of the universe arising out of the freedom which God has conferred upon it in his creation. Far from being incompatible with the transcendent freedom of God it is creatively and continuously sustained by him as a creaturely reflection of his own. This correlation of the freedom of the universe with the unlimited freedom of the Creator enters into the very core of contingent intelligibility and the kind of spontaneous order that it yields in nature, which we are unable to anticipate by any kind of a priori method operating with logico-causal continuities.

Let us come at this from a slightly different angle, in an extension of a point that emerged toward the end of the previous chapter.[16] Since there is no reason in the universe why it had to be this particular universe, for it might have been otherwise, its actualization as this universe of ours must be thought of as one of numberless possibilities. Moreover, if the actualization of that possibility took place not through any necessitation in God but through the free act of his beneficent will, the actual universe cannot be thought of as yielding its secrets to us under the coercion of our logico-deductive operations. Thus from a purely theoretical approach, in which we are concerned only with conceivable possibilities, we are unable to decide which possibility is the right and true one, that is, which is intrinsic to the actual reality of our world. There is only one regular way of discovering that, by testing the various possibilities we think up for empirical appropriateness. Thus, for example, in determining some physical law we may be able to produce several different formulations of it, all of which are theoretically equally acceptable, but the one alternative we finally choose, to the exclusion of all others, we choose under the compulsion of empirical evidence, for it is finally nature itself alone that can disclose to us its hidden pattern and thus be the judge of the truth or falsity of the many possible theories we bring to it.[17] What lies behind this remarkable openness of nature to a variety of possible interpretations is the contingence of the universe upon the unlimited rationality and freedom of the Creator. If that contingence makes the universe mysterious and baffling, it is not because it is deficient in rationality but rather because the extent and nature of its rationality exceed our capacity to achieve complete mastery over it and therefore to reach any final formalization of it. It is through being correlated to the endless possibilities of the Creator, that the universe is endowed with innate power constantly to surprise us in its manifestation of unexpected features and structures which nevertheless always turn out to be consistent with its other features and structures. What else is that but a manifestation of its contingent intelligibility and indeed its objective reality over which we have no control? This intelligibility of the created universe, its intrinsic orderliness, consistency, and reliability, is the ground of our confidence in scientific inquiry, but it is the contingent nature of that intelligibility which makes the universe attract and challenge the most arduous and unremitting scientific effort, and gives discovery its immense excitement.

When we turn to ask how modern science since Galileo and Newton has reacted to this Christian conception of contingence, we find it exhibiting a rather ambivalent attitude toward it. That is understandable in view of the two-fronted character of contingence which we have been discussing: its orientation toward God and away from him, its radical dependence and independence. The idea of a dependent independence is not easy in any case, but it was made particularly difficult by assumptions of Greek thought that lingered on into the modern period. On the other hand, the fundamental place of contingency in the presuppositions and in the day-to-day pursuit of modern science is unquestionable. This is particularly apparent in the radically different approach to nature now emancipated from the domination of rationalist thought for independent investigation, the new kind of question put to nature in order to let it disclose itself to experimental inquiry so that science may operate only with the rationality inherent in nature, the reliance throughout upon empirical evidence as utterly essential and not in any sense optional, and thus the all-important interdependence of theory and experiment which so sharply differentiates modern science from its predecessors.[18]

At the same time the acceptance of the contingent, autonomous nature of the world called for the development of autonomous modes of scientific inquiry appropriate to it. This involved what might be called a 'methodological secularism', i.e. an orientation in which science bracketed the world off from its relation to God, in order to investigate its nature for its own sake. That was certainly in line with the renewed stress of the Reformation upon God's creation of the world out of nothing, and of the primacy of his grace in which God turns toward the world he has made, which summons man to join him in that movement of his grace toward the world, and that had the effect of making natural scientific investigation of the world part of man's obedience to the Creator. Before long, however, this new orientation toward an autonomous world gave rise to extensive secularization. That is to say, the methodological secularism which natural science implies over-reached itself and gave way to dogmatic secularism. Thus there was brought about the climate in which many modern people have found it rather difficult to accept contingence in any radical form, for as soon as the dependence of the universe upon the Creator is pushed aside, the independence of the world tends to arrogate to itself the status of a wholly self-supporting and self-explaining necessary system. In the course of such a development an over-rationalizing of autonomous scientific method easily pushes empirical science into empiricism in which it tumbles back into rationalism. That is evidently what lies behind the temptation of our modern science constantly to resolve contingence away. And what is that but something like sawing off the branch one is sitting on?

E.L. Mascall has pointed his finger here at the relativity-physicists who have shown themselves 'only too ready to succumb to the tendency to apriorism'.[19] So far as Einstein himself was concerned we find a studied balance between deduction and experience. On the one hand he could say that the supreme task of the physicist is 'to arrive at those elementary laws from which the cosmos can be built up by pure deduction',[20] and on the other hand insist that 'experience remains, of course, the sole criterion of the physical utility of a mathematical construction'.[21] The immense drive toward logical unification in the field of physics, together with logical economy and simplicity,[22] laid relativity-physics open to temptation to apriorism, in that it considerably widens the gap between the theoretical structure of general relativity and verifiable consequences, or between the axioms and the empirical facts.[23] It is in this way that one must view the scientific drive toward ever more complete rationalization found in the work of mathematical physicists and astrophysicists like Eddington and Milne, in a deductive recasting of empirically gained knowledge of the cosmos, which had the effect of reimposing upon the immanent relations of the cosmos patterns of necessity and thereby obscuring its contingent nature.[24]

This problematic attitude to contingence may be traced back to the Newtonian foundations of modern science, in the discovery of how to convert empirical phenomena into quantifiably calculable results so that a deductive systematization of empirically gained knowledge would be possible. Actually, of course, Newton's scientific method involved a twofold movement, in moving deductively through experiments from observational phenomena to principles and propositions, and then in relating them back again, demonstratively through other experiments, to observational phenomena.[25] However, as J.D. Bernal has expressed it, 'he was careful in the *Principia* to recast all the work in the form of classical Greek geometry understandable by other mathematicians and astronomers.'[26] As we have suggested at an earlier point, this had the effect of obscuring the dynamic account of the universe which he achieved by encasing it in a rigid framework of static relations independent of time. Thus while it is undoubtedly the case that for Newton himself science had to do with contingent relations and states of affairs in the actual universe of bodies in motion, and was dedicated to the establishing of rigorous knowledge of that universe through experimental questioning of nature and consistent, critical handling of empirical evidence, he left his successors with a mathematical method of mechanizing the phenomena of nature from the framework of an antecedently conceived system of geometrically defined premises and axioms which, because of its immense success in Newton's *System of the World* and his declared rejection of 'hypotheses',[27] was taken as the cue for a rigorously deductivist development of scientific method. Thus what emerged in the history of Newtonian science was a hard mechanistic system, a rigid determinism of physical law which undermined the contingent foundations of natural science, not to speak of its sharp conflict with the freedom of the scientist himself. This is not to say that the pursuit of experimental science slackened: on the contrary, but it was often regarded as a preliminary stage on the way to the establishment of necessary causal relations which could be achieved only by way of abstracting from contingent states of affairs. Here we have evidence of a tendency in the scientific mind within a dualist disjunction between the theoretical and the empirical, to overstress the theoretical to the detriment of the empirical ingredient in knowledge. The formal element in our observations is isolated and detached, erected into a nomistic structure, and then imposed prescriptively upon nature.

That tendency was even stronger in the empiricist science of Ernst Mach and the theoretical physicists who with him fell under the influence of Kant,[28] according to whom laws of nature are not read out of nature but read into nature.[29] Kant clearly had no room in his thought for contingent intelligibility in any authentic sense, so that it is not surprising that he should have tried to rationalize contingency away. The 'contingent' or 'accidental' (*zufällig*), he argued, far from excluding necessity, implies it, for the contingent refers to that which is necessary under a condition.[30] Since the contingent exists only in a series of causal connections between contingent events reaching back to what is unconditionally necessary, contingence is only a manifestation, at two or more removes, of necessity. This really represents a lapse back into the old Greek conception of contingence as having an in-built relation to necessity. In this context that would mean that contingence in the universe is found only under condition of a necessary relation to physical law. But actually the reverse seems to be the case; that physical law is to be regarded as obtaining only under conditions of contingency in the universe, otherwise physical laws would have to be cut off from the contingent basis upon which natural science rests, which would make them empirically irrelevant. That is to say, relevant physical laws are themselves finally contingent.

The ambivalent attitude to contingence, and the difficulty of breaking free from the contingence-necessity syndrome, are very evident in problems raised by quantum theory. I have in mind particularly the cognate notions of indeterminacy and uncertainty made so prominent in the Göttingen form of quantum theory, and the questions they roused. Is the unpredictability of a particle of light, bound up with the fact that precise determinations of its position and of its momentum at a given time conflict with one another, only the result of our inability as yet to get at causal connections irrespective of ourselves as observers and the distorting interference of our measuring instruments, or is it inherent in reality and therefore to be accepted as a fundamental feature of nature to be taken into account in all physical law? If that feature is to be defined as 'indeterminacy', is that not to renounce the principle of causality? In other words, is nature characterized after all by chance elements that bear no relation to necessity, or is chance at the atomic level to be rationalized through reference to a deeper necessity at the sub-atomic level?

The ambivalence that marks these questions is enlighteningly reflected in the friendly clash of opinion between Einstein and Born.[31] Einstein's rejection of chance was interpreted by Born as a lapse into determinism, but, as Pauli rightly showed him, Einstein was not a 'determinist' but a 'realist'.[32] Natural science, as Einstein understood it, is dedicated to the apprehension and description of realities themselves, and not merely of the probability of their occurrence, far less of our observations of their occurrence. And since all knowledge of reality starts with experience and ends in experience, science must operate with basic concepts and principles that are empirically grounded and which, when they are made the basis for deductive reasoning, must not be abstracted from their empirical content. That is why science cannot properly operate with ideas that are merely deductively derived or are the offspring of logical necessity. The recognition of that fact, Einstein claimed, really came home to him only with the general theory of relativity which took into account a wider range of empirical facts, and in a more satisfactory and complete way, than was possible on a Newtonian basis.[33] Hence in quantum theory Einstein called for much the same kind of continuous, dynamic relatedness inherent in reality as had forced itself on him in relativity theory, but that meant operating with a very different conception of rational order for which the chance-necessity dialectic was irrelevant. God does not play dice, but he does not wear his heart on his sleeve. God is subtle but not malicious: he does not play tricks on us.[34]

Einstein's views apart, what relation does indeterminacy bear to contingence? Certainly the notion of indeterminacy seems to be conceivable only with reference to a system characterized by determinacy, in this case classical mechanics. That would imply that indeterminacy and determinacy are the obverse of one another, each delimiting and negatively defining the other on the same logical level. Is indeterminacy then only an approximation to determinacy, that is, contingence in the Kantian sense of what is held under conditions of causality and necessity? Quite evidently for Heisenberg at any rate, something more than that was intended: a real feature in nature which is not explicable within the terms of a causalist and necessitarian system because it falls outside the states of affairs to which causal and necessary laws apply.[35] But the questions still remain. Does indeterminacy refer to something quite random and arbitrary and therefore unintelligible? If it does the very foundations of science are put in question, so that it would be natural for scientists to react in favour of the view that 'contingency' only arises in their minds when they are unable as yet to reduce everything in that universe to causal laws, which would imply that they believe that the notion of contingence would progressively disappear the more progress they made along those lines. But that, once more, would cut away the empirical foundations of natural science. On the other hand, if indeterminacy does not refer to something quite random and arbitrary, does it not refer to an *intelligible contingent relation* requiring for its elucidation a different set of operational principles? In this event 'indeterminacy' (however misleading the term itself may be) must be regarded as implying that the operational principles of classical mechanics, formalized as physical laws, have only a limited range and validity, but that they may be related to the required new set of operational principles much as the principle of non-contradiction in logic is related to the wider and richer principle of sufficient reason. That is to say, physical laws must be formulated under conditions of contingence, where contingence is held not as an essential presupposition but as a constitutive factor in the structure of all natural law.

There are two questions here that demand further consideration.

1. Initial conditions. Classical physics had already recognized these as inexplicably given factors, contingent (for they might well have been different) and yet unique (for once they are given they cannot be undone). Laws were formulated under conditions of these contingent factors, but they were treated only as presuppositions that could not be included in the explanatory structure of physical laws, for as unique they were not subject to the processes of generalization entailed in the formalization of laws. However, in a finite and expanding universe in which *time* enters as an essential ingredient into its empirical reality, the questions why there are initial conditions rather than not, and why the initial conditions are what they are, cannot be avoided. That is to say, the initial conditions, singularities though they are, are also boundary conditions that bear upon an intelligible ground beyond themselves, and that require this meta-empirical reference to be consistently and intelligibly integrated with the universe, upon the nature of which they have such a decisive influence. In virtue of that consistency and intelligibility should not initial, contingent conditions be treated as fundamental factors in the structure of our physical laws, which might help us to understand, up to a point at least, why they take the form they do?

2. Accidental features. If we are concerned with an intelligible relation in nature to which the dialectic of chance-necessity, indeterminacy–determinacy, is not properly applicable, then the concept of the 'accidental' needs to be rethought on an objective ground of its own. I have in mind here a remark of Heisenberg with reference to the kind of accident which plays so important a role in Darwinian theory, that accident may be 'something very much subtler than we think'.[36] The problem of accident or chance in Darwinian theory, to which Heisenberg did not allude, is that it is indissolubly tied into a mechanical or determinist

explanation of natural selection, which means that the apparently immense stress upon sheer contingence is not what it seems. Indeed the whole concept of accidental selection and formation is a 'logical muddle' for what is demonstrated is not the survival of the fit but the non-survival of the unfit, that is, that purely accidental collocations do not yield any positive ordering principle.[37] The appeal which we are frequently tempted to make in various fields to an infinite number of chance events or accidental variations to account for the emergence of a new phenomenon in nature, is often little more than the imposition of a 'black box' on the really significant connections (which is a way of not thinking of their internal order) and seems inevitably to lead to a determinist result. It would appear that in the long run, resort to so-called 'probability-laws' and 'chance-laws' in a merely statistical resolution of the problem of 'indeterminacy' or 'uncertainty' would have a similar result, and so fail to uncover any objective dynamic order in contingent events and relations. That was, of course, Einstein's objection. Certainly we are not likely to grasp any such objective dynamic order if at the back of our minds we still operate with a chance-necessity dialectic.

Two things would seem to be required. On the one hand, a way of thinking in which what appeared to be 'accidental' would be coordinated with a higher level of order which would give it coherence and intelligibility, 'scrambling out', as it were apparent irrationalities or otherwise indecipherable sets of events, without any reductionist lapse back into causalism or determinism. That seems to have been the intention of Heisenberg when he claimed that the 'accidental' was rather more subtle than we imagined, and which, interestingly, he coordinated with what he called 'the central order of things' and likened to the notion in Einstein's mind when he spoke of 'God'.[38] On the other hand, there is needed a way of thinking in which we take the *trajectory of temporal motion* into our basic equations at all levels, which might enable us not only to grasp the subtle, natural cohesion in contingent events and relations, but also offer some account of the remarkable one-way processes throughout the universe whether at microscopic or macroscopic levels, and not least the equally remarkable ascending direction that characterizes evolution of nature or the expansion of the universe toward ever more flexible and open forms of rational order, which chance and necessity cannot begin to cope with. Here we would have a dynamic principle of intelligible order, without determinism, making for increasing innovation, richness of organization, and freedom in terms of which natural laws could be formulated in such a way that they did not conflict with the freedom of the scientific enterprise itself!

Let us now consider these possibilities from a different perspective by returning to a point made earlier, that in an outlook characterized by cosmological and epistemological dualism, we are apt to overstress the theoretical ingredient in knowledge, and lapse into empiricism and rationalism. In these circumstances mathematics through a process of idealization may easily acquire an autonomous tautological status detached from empirical reality, which inevitably creates difficulties for our understanding and interpretation of contingence and contingent intelligibility in the universe. The problem does not lie with mathematics as such, but with the external way in which it is brought to bear upon relations in nature. Properly regarded, of course, mathematics arises out of nature itself, but its elaboration into a formal or symbolic system through processes of abstraction and generalization has the effect of detaching it from nature. It is through the development of symbolic systems of this kind that the power and range of our mental capacities are greatly increased. Thus through mathematical structures we are able to penetrate more deeply into the determinate relations of the physical world and at the same time to push our grasp of those relations beyond the limits of our ordinary ways of thought and speech. Mathematics, therefore, is much more than an effective method for the deductive clarification of what we already know, for it has an enormous heuristic power in disclosing structures in the intelligible universe of which we would otherwise have to remain quite ignorant. Mathematics has this heuristic power, however, in so far as it remains what Clerk Maxwell called 'embodied mathematics',[39] that is, for all its necessary measure of detachment as a symbolic system, a mathematics that retains its natural bond with nature, for it is precisely through an intimate relation between mathematical formalization and physical theory that mathematics is such a powerful servant of scientific discovery and coherent scientific knowledge. In all this idealization has a significant part to play in the simplification of our knowledge of states of affairs which enables us to grasp their all-important rational connections apart from obstructing irrelevances. However, just as abstraction leading to a damaging detachment of mathematics from nature can hinder discovery, so idealization which leads us to disregard more subtle relations can hold up the advance of scientific knowledge. That is what happens when mathematics is allowed to degenerate into a tautological system which is only obliquely related to the real world of empirical reality. In so far as mathematics is regarded, for all its immense sophistication, as essentially a conceptual tool derived from nature and pointing us back to nature, it fulfils its supreme and altogether essential role, but as such it is a formalism through which the scientist thinks and not one that cramps or determines his thought.

Nevertheless problems arise, and have arisen in the history of thought, which require critical vigilance on the part of mathematical physicists. Two main points come to mind. On the one hand, a problem may arise out of the fact that mathematics is committed to the procedure in which states of affairs in experienced reality are analysed into discrete particles or digital units which have to be represented as identical—hence whatever does not fit into this *Gleichschaltung* may be ignored as an irrelevant contingency! Through their symbolic representations these units are ordered in respect of their relative positions to one another and grouped into sets of identities or equations which can be formulated according to sets of rules. This may have the effect of dissolving out of our thought objective connections in nature and therefore of letting actual change or motion slip through the mathematical mesh or system brought to interpret them.[40] It was certainly through the application of the infinitesimal calculus to deal with movement and change in nature that the science of dynamics achieved its staggering successes in arriving at the laws of motion and altering the whole perspective in man's understanding of the universe from a static to a dynamic approach. Nevertheless, the question must be asked: how far was classical physics able to cope with the actual flow of time or with continuous motion, and how far was it able to cope only with the acceleration of motion, or the change in the rate of change, which might be represented in precise mathematical calculations? This is the question now being put to classical physics and mechanics by the advocates of the thermodynamics of open systems—systems that cannot be understood from a fixed base or a completely given set of conditions, for any understanding must reckon with the spontaneous emergence of extra factors in which temporal becoming is given an integral place. According to Prigogine, in classical physics 'change is nothing but a denial of becoming, and time is only a parameter, unaffected by the transformation which it describes. . . . Motion is decomposed into states whose succession—whether considered in the past or in the future with respect to time—is governed by a deterministic mathematical law.'[41] In this event, classical mathematization of dynamic relations has yielded a necessitarian view of the universe which eliminates contingence.

On the other hand, a problem arises in connection with the fact that mathematics is committed to processes of classification and generalization. In employing a fixed notation to supposit for realities or states of affairs in nature, mathematics singles out those features which they have in common so that they can be correlated into classes for which suitable symbolic expressions are given. The same process is carried out into further stages until various classes are generalized into one comprehensive class, the symbolic expression for which is held to be universally valid for all classes concerned and their component units. Thus mathematical generalization tends to have the effect of rubbing out of reckoning the differentiating features and singularities of the empirical world and of throwing up a highly abstract uniformity. Such a process is methodologically necessary, but it must be recognized to have its limitations.[42] In the final analysis mathematical representation and generalization cannot yield more than probabilities, more than approximations or descriptions that are limiting cases, so that mathematical explanations in the nature of the case are partial explanations.[43] When that is forgotten and mathematical sequences and measurements are not distinguished from the empirical connections and structures in nature to which they are symbolically correlated and which they are deployed to interpret, they have the effect of imposing upon nature an artificial homogeneity. The same problem arises, of course, with formal or symbolic logic, which is the logic of class inclusion and exclusion, and as such is the logic of homogeneity. Hence, as Elsasser has argued, if wrongly applied it can hinder our understanding of real connections in nature where, in organic structures and relations above all, we require something like a logic of inhomogeneity.[44] The difficulty we have to reckon with, therefore, is the fact that the abstract uniformity inherent in the mathematical method, if allowed more than a formal methodological role in scientific thought, will tend to resolve away all contingence.

Some qualification of this argument is needed, however, for this is not precisely what happens, or what only rarely happens. Even in a profoundly dualist orientation such as we find in Newtonian science, mathematics remained, albeit in an external way, allied to nature, so that mathematical generalization could deploy among its axioms basic ideas and principles derived from nature, as Newton insisted.[45] It was of course the logical derivation of those ideas from nature, as Einstein argued, which damaged the relation between mathematics and nature in the Newtonian system.[46] Be that as it may, the universe is so thoroughly contingent in its nature that natural phenomena are regularly found capable of various theoretical interpretations which, as we have seen, may be equally valid, while mathematical symbolization is so powerful that it can elaborate, even on the basis of axioms connected with nature, theorems and constructions which, while logically consistent and elegant in themselves, far outrun, not simply the level of knowledge gained at the time, but the inherent structures of nature. Hence, as we have also seen, a choice between various mathematical possibilities must be made. This is why, in Einstein's words, 'the development of physics has shown that at any given moment, out of all conceivable constructions, a single one has always proved itself decidedly superior to all the rest.[47]

Now in generating formalizations of great comprehensiveness, which we identify with laws of nature claimed to be universally and timelessly valid, are we not confusing comprehensiveness with universality and turning natural laws into necessary truths of reason? If on the other hand we accept only mathematical formalizations which are found to be relevant to empirical states of affairs and indeed to concrete instances, then do we not thereby acknowledge that they have a limited or finite validity, and that as natural laws they may be held only under conditions of contingency? Judging by the history of modern thought, difficulties for empirical science arise whenever mathematics is treated as constituting a tautological system at the expense of damaged relations with the real world. But whenever mathematics is regarded as intimately correlated with the structures of the empirical universe through *open-textured* or *incomplete symbols*, then by its realist nature it is found to have a *reference outside its own system* which limits the validity of its formalizations. That insight ranges across modern science from Pascal to Gödel.

No one realized this more clearly than Einstein. He was deeply aware of the problems created by the idealizing operations of mathematics and by the fact that mathematical representation involves reduction in the empirical content of our scientific ideas, but he was also deeply convinced that only a definite connection with experience can give cognitive value to our systems of concepts. Thus he disposed of the lofty artificial framework of absolute mathematical time and space erected by classical physics, and grounded the framework of physics in the dynamic relatedness that permeates the actual universe in which conceptual and empirical elements are so closely combined that it is not easy to distinguish them.[48] I think particularly here of his lecture before the Prussian Academy of Sciences in 1921 in which he argued that geometry and experience are so closely intertwined that geometry must be regarded as a form of 'natural science'. That is to say, geometry thus regarded constitutes the epistemological structure in the heart of physics, with which it is so indissolubly united that it cannot be isolated as an independent conceptual system complete and consistent on its own — otherwise it would be empty and irrelevant.

Two of the claims made by Einstein in that lecture are especially relevant to our present purpose: that 'in so far as the propositions of mathematics refer to reality, they are not certain; and as far as they are certain, they do not refer to reality'; and that the universe is 'finite' even if in a certain sense 'unbounded'.[49] Behind these statements lie the epistemological implications of general relativity, with its rejection of the dualist basis which separated, in principle, mathematics and empirical knowledge, and its rediscovery of the inherent unity of geometrical and physical forms in nature, and thus with the all-important indivisibility of structure and matter, or form and being, within a space-time universe that is ultimately defined with reference to the finite speed of light.[50] If this is the case, then the theoretical components in our scientific knowledge of the universe, which are grounded in its inherent structure or form, are themselves finite and limited, which forces us to recognize the limited validity of physical laws. This has been reinforced since Einstein by the realization that general relativity, while enabling startling cosmological discoveries, predicts its own limits, as it were, which is evident, for example, when we read the expansion of the universe backwards to zero points of time and space, or when the equations of relativity come up against the limitations of so-called 'black holes' before which our physical laws, as indeed at all zero points, become critical. Far from detracting from the immense worth of relativity theory this serves only to establish its validity but within a limited range demanded by it.

These developments entitle us to ask certain basic questions. If mathematical propositions bearing upon empirical reality are not certain, and if the physical laws which they enable us to formalize are limited, then will not final formalization of physical law be impossible, for we are up against limits of a theoretical as well as an empirical kind, i.e. contingent intelligibility, inherent in the universe and deriving from its initial conditions over which we have no control? Further, if this is the case, do we not have to recognize the impossibility of any *final formal unification* of physical law? This is not to depreciate Einstein's long search for a unified field theory, if by that is meant a comprehensive theory within which gravitation theory, quantum theory and thermodynamic theory are combined together, and through which we transcend the obstructive dualism of particle and field. Indeed perhaps we are now on the way toward that end through new advances in particle theory in which particles and force-fields are onto-relationally interconnected, or in thermo-dynamic theory now applied to open or non-equilibrium systems yielding a really dynamic view of the universe, and through the startling theory put forward by Stephen Hawking of quantum-mechanical emissions from so-called 'black holes' which would seem to combine quantum and gravitation theory,[51] not to mention the recent reports of gravitation waves in line with Einstein's predictions. But even so could we ever reach anything more than a coordinated series of equations linking all physical laws, with the recognition at the same time, that in the nature of the case in a finite universe formalizations of physical laws bearing upon reality are necessarily inexact and limited? As Richard Feynman has expressed it, with all our laws 'there is always an edge of mystery, always a place where we have some fiddling to do'.[52] He adds, however, that this may be due to a lack of knowledge and not to a property of nature, but it is difficult to agree with this rider if the universe is finite and the Gödelian theorems are valid. Thus the utmost we might expect would be a deeper grasp of what physical structures have in common and a deeper understanding of the internal interactions and harmonious relations that obtain among them, with considerable simplification of basic laws, yet without being able finally to formalize the ultimate stabilizing and regularising force of cohesion throughout all physical structures. This is not to admit that in the last analysis the universe is lacking in unity or reliability, but that its intelligi-bility is of a contingent kind characterized by measures of freedom and spontaneity that do not allow of the sort of predictability which we are tempted to look for through our mathematical projections and necessities. That quality has little to do with 'indeterminacy' but rather to do with the astonishing capacity of the universe to reveal itself to us in an ever widening and deepening range of future disclosures requiring from us quite new ways of thinking and new laws of a more flexible and subtle nature, a quality which, as Michael Polanyi has shown so frequently, is a fundamental aspect of the reality of the universe. Such subtle intelligibility or such immense wealth of form, defying the possibility of final formalization, would not characterize the universe if it were ultimately necessary, for necessity at the back of everything would only stereotype or standardize all patterns in nature, and what a dull universe that would be!

This line of thought seems considerably strengthened by the fact that *time* has forced its way back into the essential subject-matter of scientific knowledge—that is, not time in the Newtonian sense which was broken down into timeless points whose sequence was regarded as governed by necessary mathematical law (where a way of measuring 'time' appears to substitute for time), but real time in Bergson's sense as a feature and function of the on-going empirical world. I think here in the first instance of the point made by V. F. Weisskopf in his 1975 presidential lecture to the American Academy of Science on 'The Frontiers and Limits of Science', that atoms and molecules and nuclei all reveal a history, for time enters into what they now actually are.[53] That does not apply, he claims, to protons, neutrons, and electrons which have no intrinsic properties revealing what happened to them in the past, but it does apply particularly to all self-reproducing structures from the smallest to the largest organisms, for their evolution is written into what they now are and are still in process of becoming. That is to say, the history of matter enters into our scientific understanding of it. I think in the second instance here of the work of Ilya Prigogine and his colleagues in connection with the extension of thermodynamic theory beyond its classical frame of reference to non-equilibrium or open systems, in such a way as to account for the rise of new dynamic states of matter deriving from irreversible processes, and of a new kind of organization which spontaneously emerges out of apparently random fluctuations far from a state of equilibrium.[54] Incidentally, it is also shown that non-equilibrium order offers the possibility of a new variational principle in evolution replacing the determinist principle of Darwinian theory.[55] What concerns us at the moment, however, is that here time is given its full meaning associated with irreversibility within spontaneously arising structures, and does not merely appear as a geometric parameter externally associated with motion. We have a new kind of time-dependent functional order coordinating space–time to the dynamic processes within the system, and a non-unitary transformation theory is developed to enable a move from a thermodynamic to a genuinely dynamic account of nature. In this way once more an historical element is introduced even into physico-chemical description of processes in the universe.

This thermodynamic recovery of real time clearly relates to and reinforces the realization that time has an integral place in the expansion of the universe initiated by the immense explosion from its incredibly dense state some 20 to 15 billion years ago. The empirical evidence resulting from this, the so-called fossil radiation discovered by Penzias and Wilson in 1965, would seem to put a fatal question to the speculative theories which in one way or another offer an oscillating or a cyclic, i.e. a necessary, account of the universe, and to confirm the fact that the universe is finite in origin and in time and space, inherently temporal and limited.[56] Thus the expansion of the universe is to be regarded as a vast temporal singularity, in fact an immense unique historical event characterized by irreversibility. This has the effect of destroying the old rationalist dichotomy between accidental truths of history and necessary truths of reason, and of calling in question the rationalist idea that science is finally concerned only with timeless and necessary truth, for now it seems even more evident that all scientific truths and all physcial laws, which belong to and emerge with the expansion of the finite universe, are as contingent as the universe itself.

Now it is evidently due to the irreversibility of time that contingent events which do not happen out of necessity nevertheless have a form of 'necessity', and indeed of 'necessary consistence', in the sense that once they have taken place they are what they are and cannot be otherwise, which applies also to their contingent sequences. It would be a fatal mistake to confuse this with the hard necessity of logical consistency or determinism, according to which the events had to happen as they did. That fallacy arises from an illusion created by reading the end-result of the sequence back along the line of happening into the beginning, which is inevitable when we reverse and logicalize the cause–effect relation in a syllogistic manner, thus tracing the conclusion back to the premises. However, it is in virtue of contingent necessity and consistency that, once we have discovered structures or

sequential patterns of contingent intelligibility in the expanding universe which we could not have predicted, we can
throw our dynamic understanding of them into a static
deductive order, with a view to simplifying our grasp of the
connections involved by formalizing away distracting irrel-
evancies. An instance of this has been provided by Victor
Weisskopf in which he has shown that in terms of six given
factors, the mass of the proton, the mass and electrical
charge of the electron, the velocity of light, Newton's
gravitational constant, and the quantum of action, it is
possible to express all the relevant magnitudes which characterize the properties of matter, such as the density and
hardness of matter, the height of mountains, the visibility
of compact matter, and the size of a star.[57]

It is owing to contingent 'necessity' and consistency which
characterize the universe that this kind of mathematical
calculation can be made, which serves simplification and
unification in our knowledge of the physical world, but it
is important to bear in mind the inherent limits that such
procedures and indeed all scientific analysis involve, of
which Weisskopf is particularly aware. Were we not to
follow him in that respect we would sin against thermodynamic irreversibility and the unidirectionality of time,
resolving away contingence and converting a dynamic and
consistently monotonic account of the expanding universe
into a non-dynamic and necessitarian account. The universe
increasingly manifests itself to our inquiries as an open
intelligible system, not one whose immanent processes are
closed necessarily upon themselves, requiring from us open-
structured modes of thought and formulation to match its
nature.[58] As inadequacies and obstructive rigidities become
manifest in its theories and formalizations, science looks for
a more subtle handling of mathematics and a more flexible
formulation of physical law in order to do justice to the
inherent spontaneity and dynamism of nature. Thus through
constant modification theories and laws are kept open
toward further disclosures of the universe which could not
be anticipated by the logical structure of prior knowledge.

Throughout this discussion I have been arguing from a
number of angles that the scientific enterprise and the
contingent universe are correlates, for that enterprise is

itself part of the expanding universe. The intelligibility of the universe provides science with its confidence, but the contingence of the universe provides science with its challenge. It is this deep intertwining of contingence and intelligibility that lies behind the characteristic interdependence of experiment and theory that has marked modern science since Galileo. Whenever the relation between contingence and intelligibility is damaged, science is tempted to move in a rationalizing direction in which its conceptual machinery develops an autonomy and a momentum of its own, but again and again the advance of scientific inquiry is brought to a halt before unpredictable elements in nature, revealing a profounder and more sophisticated form of organization and calling for a deepening of the scientific enterprise in which the empirical and theoretical components are more tightly woven together to match the indivisible unity of contingence and intelligibility in nature.

Today we have reached the point where scientific investigation of the universe has come up against its finiteness and temporality in the strongest way, while trying to grasp the universe as an intelligible whole. More and more science knocks at the very boundaries of existence, empirical and theoretical boundaries, where the staggering intelligibility of its own enterprise gives rise to the profoundest questions and which it will not allow to be stifled. The intelligibility inherent in the universe indicates far more than is actualized in its processes or can be formalized in natural laws, and correspondingly the intelligibility generated in the scientific enterprise points to a dimension of intelligibility transcending it compared to which it appears relatively elementary. Thus the coordinated intelligibilities of the universe and of our scientific knowledge of it demand justification for themselves of a meta-empirical and meta-scientific kind, for without that they would finally be meaningless and pointless.

In traditional thought this intelligible reference of the universe beyond itself has been construed not in a semantic but in a logical way, and formulated as an argument through the principle of sufficient reason from the contingent nature of the world to a non-contingent, necessary ground in God. The difficulty with that argument is that such a correlation of contingence with necessity has the effect of finally necessitating down the line every contingent connection leading to it, as indeed Kant saw so clearly, thus in the last analysis resolving contingence away—the fallacy of Greek and all rationalizing science. The classical form of this argument was provided by Leibniz, who regarded contingence as something not properly capable of analysis in itself, like an irrational number which can nevertheless be reasonably handled within an infinite series which terminates in the mind of God, the ultimate ground of all certainty, necessity, and rationality. The curious thing is that Leibniz devised the principle of sufficient reason to cope intelligibly with the combination of reason and contingence in motion and operation which the principle of non-contradiction was incapable of doing, but in the last resort his mathematicization or logicalization of the connections led him back into the toils of necessitarianism. That form of the reference of intelligibility of the created universe beyond itself only lands in stultification.

There is no reason, however, why the argument should be logicalized, any more than we are obliged to operate with a logical relation between the empirical reality of the universe and our scientific understanding of it—the fallacy that Einstein destroyed so effectively.[59] Within the framework of the scientific enterprise the intelligibility alike of the universe and of that enterprise lays hold of our minds in a way that we cannot rationally resist, calling for a sufficient reason beyond it which is not only congruous with it but requires a contingent order as its intelligible counterpart. Thus we are finally brought back through intelligible contingent relations to the constitutive relation between God the Creator and the contingent universe, the realization of which made the enterprise of empirical science possible in the first place, and actually set it on the course of its great achievements.

However, if we are to take contingence seriously, without resolving it away, we must face the baffling fact that precisely because of the contingent nature of the universe and of scientific knowledge, the reference of their intelligibilities beyond themselves breaks off, so that the questions they raise cannot terminate upon the transcendent intelligible ground they require in order to constitute the intelligibilities they actually are. Moreover, unless those intelligibilities are completed beyond themselves, the very questions they raise cannot be properly and consistently formulated, for the basic form which our knowledge takes within the autonomous universe (i.e. its contingent independence of God) inevitably turns away from its own ultimate ground in God, and thereby distorts and misdirects the questions that arise. What is needed is something like a Gödelian theorem of the universe as an intelligible whole or of the scientific enterprise as an intelligible whole, but that would still not carry us on to the actual transcendent ground from which all our intramundane knowledge would gain its ultimate consistence or coherence.[60] It would be very different if the symmetries of our intramundane intelligibilities were broken and intersected by a symmetry of a higher order, which would give them a deeper texture of intelligible meaning, for then the questions raised would be reshaped and redirected toward their proper end in God the Creator of the universe.

This is an orientation of thought that one would expect to find mediated through an interaction between natural science and theological science, for theology arises out of the intersection of our human experience and knowledge by divine revelation which thereby takes root in them and opens them out upward toward God. As such the concern of theology for the world is not so much with its contingence away from God, which is the preserve of natural science, but with its contingence on God, and thus it is the science that is unable to halt at the limits that would otherwise satisfy natural science. But since it is precisely the contingence of the realities of the empirical universe upon God that gives them their intelligibility and enables us to grasp their natural and inherent connections, genuine interaction between theological science and natural science cannot but be helpful to both. Of primary importance for natural science is the doctrine of the creation of the universe out of nothing, for in it a new thought world, while having no logical continuity with the thought world arising out of our natural sciences, establishes continuity with it and coordinates it with a higher order of meaning in which its own level of meaning is all the more firmly established. Far from detracting from the contingent, autonomous status of the universe, which makes natural science a requirement of the creation, it reinforces our understanding of contingence and of empirical inquiry. That is why closer dialogue between natural science and theological science may help science to remain rigorously faithful to the contingent nature of the universe and its intelligibility which, as we have seen, it seems to have a recurring tendency to resolve away.

The contribution such a dialogue might make to natural science may be indicated by brief reference to two points in the foregoing discussion. In the first place, a theological understanding of the created universe as constantly sustained, regulated, and given inner cohesion through the presence of God in his creative power and rationality, may be coordinated with the search of natural science for a unified understanding of all structures and laws beyond their finite limits. Thus both theological and natural scientific understanding of the inner consistency of the empirical universe as incomplete and needing to be completed beyond the universe, would reinforce each other. In the second place, the theological understanding of the nature of intelligibility in the empirical universe as contingent upon the unlimited intelligibility of God may well help natural science to appreciate in a new way the astonishing capacity of nature to disclose ever new and unexpected forms of rational order of increasing complexity and richness of organization, without yielding to the temptation of reductionism. The grounding of the contingent intelligibility in the universe on God does not allow any equation of contingence with deficiency in rationality, but rather the reverse, for correlation with the unlimited rationality of God lends contingent intelligibility a dimension of depth that defies the possibility of complete formalization. The inherent difficulty we finite creatures have in knowing God lies in the excess of his divine rationality over our ability to comprehend it. Correlation with that rationality in God goes far to account for the mysterious and baffling nature of the intelligibility inherent in the universe, and explains the profound sense of religious awe which it calls forth from us and which, as Einstein insisted,[61] is the mainspring of science.

3

Theological and Scientific World-Views

In our day we have reached a turning-point in the history of thought at which natural science and theological science are confronted each in its own way with the need to adopt a fundamental attitude to the universe as a whole.

Natural science has always tended to generate a world-view or cosmology, such as the Ptolemaic or Copernican orientation toward the cosmos, and has since Newton been concerned to develop a system of the world; but it has also tended to renounce anything like a scientific world-view on the ground that this would mean stepping across the frontier of exact science into metaphysics, and allying itself with unwarranted cosmological presuppositions and speculations. Hence in modern times natural science has claimed to be neutral or non-committal in respect of any specific cosmology. Today, however, the situation is radically changed. On the one hand, the relentless pressure of its own inquiries has carried science to the very limits of being where it can no longer avoid the question as to initial conditions or the basic relation between concept and reality; and, on the other hand, there has steadily emerged through these inquiries an underlying conceptual unity in objective scientific knowledge ranging from microphysical to astrophysical aspects of the universe. This change is marked by the fact that there has now arisen a science of cosmology in the strict sense,[1] for the profounder our understanding of nature throughout the universe gets, the more we are forced to grapple with meta-scientific and cosmological questions and are committed to adopting a basic attitude to the universe as a whole, which cannot but affect every fundamental theory and every theory-laden experiment.

In modern times theology also has been widely concerned to abjure commitment to any specific cosmology. Some theologians, in acceptance of the Kantian and Laplacian rationalization of Newton's system of the world into a self-containing and self-explaining deterministic framework, have gone to great lengths in seeking to detach understanding of the Bible and Christian theology from any world-view, and indeed to cut off faith from any empirical correlates in physical space-time reality. Thereby, however, they have replaced a God-centred and objective outlook with a radically man-centred and subjective outlook. Other theologians who take seriously faith in God as Maker of heaven and earth, and therefore reject any conception of the universe as a self-contained and self-explanatory system, nevertheless claim that faith does not generate a distinctive view of the universe and cannot be tied up with any particular cosmology. Theology, they say, on its own proper ground, can operate freely and non-committedly within various cosmologies. Justification for this is offered on the ground that the biblical revelation does not contain any ontology of heaven and earth and is therefore not concerned with cosmology. Because theology has to do with God and man, it operates only on the cosmological border where the universe of space and time is limited by the invisible transcendent reality of the divine. On the other hand, it is admitted that faith in God as Creator of the universe implies that a cosmos detached from its Creator loses its natural axis and that man detached from the cosmos is an abstraction. Hence even on this view theology cannot operate on its own proper ground in complete detachment from cosmology.

Is it actually the case, however, that there is no distinctively biblical or Christian view of the universe? Can theology, concerned as it is with interrelations between God and man-in-the-universe, be pursued properly without consideration of its empirical correlates in the continuities and structures of space and time? It seems clear to me that both these questions must be answered in the negative. Undoubtedly faith in God finds itself restricted, if not altogether suffocated, in some cosmologies rather than in others, which implies that it cannot disregard views of the universe within the society or culture in which faith arises and seeks to take root. Likewise, theology functions more freely in some cosmologies than in others, and the fact that it may find itself in conflict—as has often happened in the past—with conceptions governing a particular outlook upon the universe, reveals that theology operates with basic cosmological conceptions of its own which it cannot give up. It is indeed distinctive of the Judaeo-Christian outlook that God interacts with man within the physical reality and order of the cosmos to which man belongs, and does not merely relate himself to man in some 'external' or 'indirect' way which could only be given mythological expression. It is in and through the medium of space and time that God acts upon man and makes himself known to him, and man is called to responsive acts of obedience and knowledge. That is to say, the fact (so essential to both Judaism and Christianity) of God's self-revelation to man within the objectivities of this empirical world carries with it spatio-temporal coefficients which faith in the living God cannot give up without defection from its foundation. By the same token theology finds itself committed to a distinctive understanding of the created order of space and time which implies basic cosmological convictions of far-reaching importance.

It is a serious fault of much modern theology with its rather one-sided emphasis on history that, while it recognizes that faith in God cannot be cut loose from temporal factors, it has nevertheless sought to cut off faith from its involvement with spatial factors. Thereby, however, theology of this sort makes faith in the God of history irrelevant for this world and renders even its own historical enterprise highly question-able, for time detached from space is empty and meaningless. This goes far to account for the current debâcle of what is called the historico-critical method in biblical interpretation, in its failure to grapple with the spatio-temporal reality of the historical Jesus, not to mention the incarnate presence and redemptive activity of God in our world of space and time.

The orientation of classical Christian theology in the early formative centuries of our era was very different, owing to the seriousness with which it took the self-revelation of God to mankind in Jesus Christ in the concrete particularities and contingencies of human existence and need. The basic under-standing of God was changed, for abstract notions of deity were replaced by concepts that were filled out with content from his saving and creative acts of grace and love in Jesus Christ. But the basic understanding of the world was also changed, for it was from the great movement of God's love to the world in Jesus Christ that they learned that the world is not only the creation of God but the object of his love and unceasing care. The incarnation brought with it the revelation that God is neither some utterly unknowable transcendent deity nor some pantheistic force immanent in the unchangeable laws of natural process. It brought instead the staggering idea that God does not hold himself aloof from the world like some unmoved mover who keeps his power to himself, but moves out of himself to become one with his creatures, while remaining what he is in all his eternal constancy as God, in such a way as to share ungrudgingly with them the power of his divine life and love in what Christians learned to call *grace*. Such an understanding of God and of his relation to the universe quickly brought Christian theology into sharp conflict with the conceptions governing the cosmologies prevailing in the ancient world, so that the great theologians were forced to make the Christian view of the world explicit and, what is more, to reconstruct the rational foundations of ancient cosmology.

We have already discussed several of these basic convictions which came eventually to bear such fruit in the rise of empirical science, and we must keep them in mind here, but let us now consider the characteristic slant of the Christian world-view from the perspective of certain aspects in the Christianized understanding of God which were given prominence in the confrontation between Christians and pagans in the different way they read the world situation. These aspects can be stated simply: God is light, God is good, and God is faithful.

God is light, said St. John, and in him there is no darkness at all. That is an idea that we are apt to take for granted, but that God is the kind of light, in fact the very Light, which shines out into the world from its embodiment in Jesus Christ, and that it is as this Light that God illumines all nature, was radically new. It was something that had to be learned in conflict with very different conceptions; that the world is determined by blind inexorable fate or sheer irrational chance, or that human existence imprisoned in the darkness of irrational matter is the prey to inscrutable occult powers that are to be feared and appeased, conceptions which lent themselves readily to magic, superstition, and astrology.

Rational Greek thought also conflicted with some of these notions through its doctrine of divine intelligible light immanent in the human reason in terms of which it was able to grasp the eternal forms embedded in the world, but, as we have seen, this was precisely the idea that ruled that there could be no empirical evidence for scientific conclusions. The Christian doctrine of God as the Light of the world was very different, in its distinction between the uncreated Light of God and the created intelligible light which is found in different forms in nature and in the human mind. It is in the light of the physical sun, which cannot be looked at in itself, that all things around us are to be seen. In itself the Light of God is inaccessible, and indeed invisible, but it is through the shining of this divine Light upon the creation that it may be known. Yet this takes place, patristic theology held, in a distinctive way: as the created and unchanging Light of God imparts to the universe, including man, a created, changeable light thereby making it everywhere intelligible and accessible to knowledge.[2] The significance of this way of expressing the idea becomes apparent when we compare it with the teaching of Plato given in the *Meno* in face of the dilemma that it is impossible for someone to inquire for what he already knows, but also impossible for him to inquire for what he does not know, for then he would not know what he was looking for and would not be able to recognize it even if he found it. Plato's solution to this 'pugnacious proposition' was given in his doctrine of *reminiscence*: all learning is ultimately a kind of recalling from within of a truth which we brought with us from a previous existence.[3] The patristic answer was very different: genuine learning is a constant discovering of the truth of things which we did not know before but which we come to know for the first time as we make actual contact with the realities concerned and know them out of their own intelligibilities.[4] That is to say, the truth into which we inquire is intimated to us by some aspect of objective reality itself and not by some preconception of our own. Thus the distinction between the uncreated Light of God and the created changeable light of nature implies that the creation is endowed with a contingent rationality of its own which is accessible to us only through empirical inquiry and through insight into what it is in itself.

We know things only as we submit our mind to the judgement of their own reality.[5] At the same time this doctrine of created light pervading the universe had the effect of exorcizing it, so to speak, of the irrationalities and arbitrary inscrutabilities with which it had been invested by man and which only served to darken his relation to the universe around him. Bathed in the Light of God that shines in concentrated form in Jesus Christ, the universe took on a radically different aspect.

The second aspect of the Christian doctrine of God we must note is his goodness, especially as it became manifest in Jesus Christ. The doctrine that in him the eternal Word of God, through whom the whole universe of visible and invisible reality was created and continues to be sustained, became incarnate, immensely reinforced the Judaic idea that the creation is essentially good because it is the handiwork of the good God. 'And God said, Let there be light: and there was light. And God saw the light, that it was good: and God divided the light from the darkness.' That theological understanding of creation deriving from the opening verses of the book of Genesis (Gen. 1:3,4), intensified through Christian belief in the goodness and integrity of the physical universe revealed in and through Jesus, played an incalculable part in transforming the ancient world-view.[6] It destroyed the Platonic and Aristotelian idea that matter is, if not evil as such, the raw material of corruption and unreality and the source of disorder in the universe,[7] and it also ruled entirely out of consideration the pessimistic views of nature that emanated from the dualist sects such as Manichaeans and Gnostics, and thereby emancipated the material reality of the universe for serious scientific attention. The incarnation had the effect of sanctifying the physical universe for God, thus requiring for it a new respect altogether, if only as the medium which God has established for communion between himself and mankind, but also as a creaturely realm of reality endowed with meaning and direction in the creative purposes of God which are yet to be consummated. Thus it was from the sheer goodness and beneficence of God, which overflowed into the world through Jesus Christ and were embodied in his physcial existence in our space and time, that Christianity learned to read the authentic nature of empirical reality, no

longer as something hostile, malevolent, or alien to the
human spirit but as the very sphere in which God's presence
has come to dwell in order to share his own glory with it.
The implications of this for a new scientific view of the
universe can be seen when we set it over against the dualist
disjunction between appearance and reality which dominated
the Hellenic mind, depreciating the sensible in comparison
with the intelligible, the phenomenal as against the noumenal,
for the doctrine of the goodness of the creation demanded
a new ontology giving authentic integrity and unity to all
creaturely and contingent being. As W.A. Whitehouse has
said so well: 'If there is to be any interpenetration of scientific thinking and theological thinking, it would seem to be the
case that this can happen only in a new formulation of
ontology'.[8]

We come now to the other aspect of the Christian doctrine
of God that is of significance for our theme, the faithfulness
of God. This is the idea that in all its creaturely fragility and
temporality the universe is harnessed to the invariance and
constancy of God's wisdom and love. Here once again the
early Christian Church took its view of the whole economy
of the space-time universe from its understanding of Jesus
Christ as the bodying forth within space and time of the
eternal purpose of God's love. That is to say, it was the
incarnation of God himself in Jesus Christ which constituted
the dynamic centre from which the whole pattern and history
of created reality is to be discerned, for all lines converge
meaningfully at that point where they are transfixed, as it
were, by a transcendent axis, much as the spokes of a cart-
wheel are made to bear upon a centre through which is thrust
the axle that gives the wheel its significance. The discovery
of the ultimate meaning and design of the universe in the
incarnation had the effect of transforming the Hebrew idea
of the covenanted mercies of God, and the Hellenic idea of
the predetermination of all things in accordance with changeless necessities, and of bringing them together in such a way
as to give rise to a thoroughly dynamic view of the cosmos
in which orderliness and temporality, regularity and novelty,
constancy and change were married together. The doctrine
of creation out of nothing had shocked the Greek mind, as
we have seen, for it appeared to throw the universe into

unstable, irrational flux, but that was to fail to see the anchoring of the time-continuum of created reality in the unswerving faithfulness and love of the Creator such as he had revealed himself to be in Jesus Christ. However, the concept of a temporal origin to the universe from such a God had the effect both of establishing the concept of the history of the physical universe as an open-ended movement which constantly takes mankind by surprise, and yet of showing that history falls within the overarching constraints of God's grace as its operation in our spatio-temporal existence is revealed in Jesus.[9] That is to say, here we have advanced a concept of the divine providence without the closed predetermination of Aristotelian final causes or the changeless natural law of the Stoics, and the concept of the creative interaction of God with the temporal order of the universe which gives rise to a new understanding of order as both real and contingent. Far from being understood in the Platonic way as a transient image of eternity, and far from being confounded with the measurement of velocity as with the Newtonians in a later age, time is filled with real content, for it is the created counterpart to the ever-new creative purposes of God himself, so that it continues to manifest from moment to moment in a dynamic present new patterns of events which could not have been anticipated from what has already happened in the past or have been predicted through any logico-deductive reasoning from abstract ideas.[10] It is this astonishing combination of unpredictability and lawfulness, not only in the history of man but in the history of all created reality in its relation to the constancy and freedom of the grace of the Creator, that lies behind the Christian conception of the cosmos as an open-ordered universe. In its correlation with the unlimited freedom and inexhaustibility of the Creator the universe is characterized neither by uncertainty nor by necessity. Far from being closed or predetermined, the universe constitutes an open-textured system in which novel forms of order constantly emerge and yet blend with what has already taken place in invariant consistency and rationality.

I have argued that this theological view of the world is read off the self-revelation of God in Jesus Christ and the Christian understanding of the interrelation of the incarnation to the creation. This implies that the natural axis of the universe is to be found not within the universe itself as an independent cosmological system, but in its relation to God its transcendent Creator. That is to say, from a theological perspective the physical universe is to be regarded as an open intelligible system which constitutes a consistent whole only in so far as it is completed beyond itself in God as its creative ground and ultimate end. This has been and no doubt will continue to be a source of friction between the theological and the natural reason, for the natural reason, rightly recognizing the autonomous (or at least semi-autonomous) status of empirical reality, constantly strives to find necessary reasons for the natural constitution of things in the universe as though it were after all a self-sufficient and a self-explanatory system — yet the very rigour of scientific method, so often demonstrated in our own times, halts that imperious drive of the autonomous reason in recognition of the limits of natural science and in increasing respect for the capacity of the natural world to disclose itself to scientific inquiry in quite unexpected ways. This is not uncongenial to theology, which from its point of view is bound to treat the material content of any purely scientific account of the universe as a partial, provisional, and revisable cosmology which can never be completed or therefore explained merely in terms of its own constituent relations but which, on its empirico-theoretical level, can nevertheless be highly meaningful for theology when it is coordinated with a higher level of rational order in God as its creative and sufficient reason. It is significant that a rigorously scientific approach to the universe today, which carries its inquiries into the immanent intelligibilities of the universe to the very boundaries of empirical reality where natural science breaks off, approximates to just such a theological understanding of it. The common factor between those two very different views of the universe, making them open to each other and such an approximation possible, is to be found in the concept of contingent order.

This concept of contingent order, however, as we have already argued, is the direct product of the Christian understanding of the constitutive relation between God and the universe, which he freely created out of nothing, yet not without reason, conferring upon what he has made and continues to sustain a created light of its own which reflects and depends upon his own uncreated Light. It was the injection of that concept into science that altered the basic view of the universe with which it worked and gave rise to the programme of continuous experimental inquiry.[11] Only in comparatively recent times, however, after the relentless advance of scientific thought in breaking through apparent barrier after barrier has brought natural science close to the limits set by the initial conditions of nature, including the finiteness of space and time, and explanations are pushed back to the ultimate assumptions or beliefs about the nature of the universe which regulate all our working scientific conceptions, has contingence been forced out into the open, compelling acknowledgement of it as an essential assumption even though it is not scientifically, far less logically, derivable, and remains, like the concept of order in the universe, un-verifiable and unfalsifiable.[12] In this event the contingent nature of the universe challenges science to reckon with it in a more positive way as an integral factor in scientific understanding and interpretation of the natural order. With that recognition the scientific world-view is bound to ap-proximate once more toward the Christian world-view which we have just been discussing. It would certainly have the effect of bringing home to us the realization that all scientific truth is contingent and limited, for it is correlated to contin-gent and limited realities, yet that should not detract from the intelligibility and validity of scientific conceptions, for scientific conceptions do not have their truth in themselves but in the realities to which they refer and on which they are grounded.

In order to help us see more clearly how the theological and scientific views of the universe may be coordinated significantly with one another, let us recall the point discussed in the second chapter that contingence has a double aspect deriving from its theological roots. On the one hand, it means that the universe depends entirely upon the grace and wisdom of God for its being and form, and is not a necessary emanation of the divine. On the other hand, it also means that the universe is given a distinctive reality of its own completely differentiated from the self-sufficient reality of God. Thus in virtue of its contingence the universe has an orientation at once toward God and away from him. Theology is more concerned with the former orientation of the universe, its dependence on God, and natural science is more concerned with the latter orientation of the universe, its independence of God—yet neither can be properly held without the other. This implies that in their basic assumptions the theological and scientific world-views are deeply interlocked.

For theology the radicalization of contingence implies that in creating the universe out of nothing God gave it a nature and order of its own which we are obliged to respect. There is theological warrant, therefore, for the independent empirical investigation of the universe by natural science—indeed such an investigation is a duty toward God laid upon us by his work of creation. For natural science the radicalization of contingence implies that the universe is endowed with an autonomous character both as a whole and throughout its immanent relations, with features and patterns and operational principles that belong to it by intrinsic natural right, such that if natural science is to be rigorously faithful to the universe that God has created it must bracket off the universe from God and develop autonomous modes of inquiry appropriate to the distinctive reality of the universe which allow it to disclose its own inherent rational order. Hence reliance upon experimental questioning, together with the forswearing of rationalistic deductivism, is a duty imposed on natural science by the contingent nature of the universe, and not an optional extra.

It is evident that theology cannot develop an adequate understanding of the relation of God to the universe which he has made without accepting the radical implications of contingence. If it does not accept them it is tempted to turn in upon itself and to treat theology as a closed rationalistic system of thought in which 'God' is defined only by reference to what man can conceive. The problem of natural science, on the other hand, is that in developing autonomous modes of scientific investigation it is tempted to treat the universe as a self-sufficient necessary system which does not need to be understood by reference outside of or beyond it. Thereby, however, natural science tends to succumb to the temptation to close in upon itself and lapse into an empiricist rationalism in which contingence is abjured and genuine empirical science is undermined. Both theological science and natural science require to respect the double aspect of contingence, dependence on God and independence from him, in order properly to be what they ought to be. Clearly theology needs dialogue with natural science to keep it properly free and open toward God, and natural science needs dialogue with theology to keep it properly free and open toward the contingent universe.

Let us explore the implications of contingent order for the coordination of natural scientific and theological world-views by injecting back into the discussion at this point the notion of contingent freedom. Just as the doctrine of God's creation of the universe out of nothing operates with a relation between the creative rationality of God and the created rationality of the universe, so it operates also with a relation between the creative freedom of God and the created freedom of the universe.[13] The combination of contingent rationality and contingent freedom, which excludes both arbitrariness and necessity, constitutes the universe an open dynamic system of contingent order in which nature is capable of a variety of possible interpretations consistent with each other, evident, as we have seen, in several equally valid formulations of some physical law. Behind this inherent openness and variability in nature lies the correlation of the rationality and freedom of the universe to the unlimited rationality and freedom and therefore to the endless possibilities of the Creator. That is to say, the combination of unpredictability and lawfulness in nature found in its capacity spontaneously to generate richer and more open-structured forms of order in the constantly expanding universe may be regarded as something like the signature of the Creator in the depths of contingent being. If contingent order of this kind manifests an indefinite range in its intelligibility which we are unable adequately to grasp, it cannot be due to any deficiency in being or intelligibility, as the ancients and mediaevals thought, but because through its correlation to the transcendent order in the Creator it exceeds our capacity to apprehend it beyond limited levels. By its very nature, however, the contingent order of the universe grips our thought in such a way that it is harnessed to a reference beyond empirical reality, when very much more is indicated to us than we can express merely in terms of intramundane relations and possibilities.

Nevertheless, if we insist on contriving for ourselves some sort of controlling formalization of what is thus indicated, we find that the truth becomes turned into a lie.[14] That is to say, the kind of intelligible order everywhere inherent in created reality contingently reflects an ultimate reality infinitely greater than we can conceive, which calls into radical question all the idolatrous surrogates of our human minds.

There is, however, another story to be told. Throughout modern times it has generally been held proper for natural science to confine itself to intramundane connections and explanations, in methodological exclusion of all reference to extramundane relations. It would seem no less proper for natural science to recognize that this exclusion is only methodological and does not imply that there is no reality beyond what is open to investigation through its own methods and instruments or is accessible to understanding and formalization within the limits of its own conceptual framework — otherwise it would be guilty of the fallacy of identifying the real with what is conceivable to the natural scientific reason alone. If this exclusion is acknowledged to be only a methodological convenience, but nevertheless remains practically in force, then it will clearly be difficult for natural science to have much to do with contingence in its double aspect as contingence away from God and contingence on God, which we have found to be essential to it.

Undoubtedly modern science does accept the idea that the universe is contingent, for that is the regulative assumption behind its reliance upon experiment and its operation with the interrelation of experiment and theory. Nevertheless science has not been without certain problems in this respect. By focussing on the determination of observable regularities in nature and their formalization as logico-causal continuities, to the exclusion of all extra-causal and extra-logical factors, science has steadily created an immensely powerful and successful conceptual machinery which has generated a momentum of its own, and functions as though it were a law to itself. In this way rigorous, exact science tends to develop a prescriptive framework from which contingence appears rather like an *absurdity* and finally baffles rational analysis, representation, and explanation.[15] Hence too frequently in on-going science contingence comes to be identified with what does not fit into exact scientific formalization and therefore to be treated as a negligible irrelevance. Thus in spite of the fact that contingence is the *sine qua non* of empirical science, there are evidently factors in modern scientific activity undermining its status and tempting science to resolve it away. On the other hand, there are factors in recent developments which reverse this trend, so that contingence once more comes into its own in a powerful way.

Factors detracting from the notion of contingent order all appear to be bound up with the view of the universe as a closed mechanistic system. For short we shall call this the 'Newtonian world-view' since Newton supplied the controlling concepts and equations, although strictly speaking it was only after Newton's time that it developed into the sophisticated deterministic outlook which dominated thought until the first quarter of the twentieth century. Basic to this view of the world was its atomism, on the one hand, and its unchanging overall structure on the other hand. All nature was regarded as comprised of separated corpuscles which even at a distance act instantaneously on one another through empty and uniform space, while retaining their substantial identity throughout all change. This enabled science to offer the possibility of an explanation of all empirical phenomena in the universe strictly in terms of mechanical causes and with precise mathematical quantification; but it had the effect of imposing artificially upon an admittedly dynamic universe of bodies in motion a rigid homogeneous framework reckoned to be needed if science is to offer an account of nature irrespective of all observers. Such an objectivist view of the world from a point of absolute rest resulted in the conception of a closed necessary order in which contingence was inevitably suppressed or at least tolerated only under condition of a necessary relation to immutable physical law.

Clearly there was a basic contradiction in the Newtonian world-view between its rigid unchanging conceptual framework, absolute time and space, and the dynamic nature of the universe which more and more came to light throughout the nineteenth century in physics and biology alike.[16] Since on these assumptions 'reality' was restricted to what can be predicted and controlled through the instruments and calculations of physics and mechanics, the gap, inherent in the dualist basis of Newtonian science, between the conceptual apparatus employed by natural science and the on-going empirical universe, widened considerably until it came to be held that science is not after all a search for reality, as Newton thought, but a necessary pragmatic device for human existence in this world, making for convenient arrangements of conceptual symbols and fictions through which we may describe scientific activity, classify observational data, and derive economical generalizations, without exerting the claim that they have any ontological bearing upon empirical reality. That is to say, an unbalanced concentration upon theoretical formalization and mathematical idealization, to the detriment of the empirical ingredient in scientific knowledge, gave rise to a positivist and conventionalist outlook in which the formulation of physical law is cut off from the ontological basis on which natural science rests, and genuine contingence is resolved away. This recurring difficulty that science, especially after Kant, Laplace, and Mach, evidently has with contingence would seem to indicate that modern science, like ancient science, by itself could not come up with the notion of contingence, but that, essential though it is to natural science, it derives from elsewhere, i.e. as we have claimed, from Christian faith.

Factors promoting the idea of contingent order are evidently bound up with the view of the universe as a unitary open system. For short we shall call this the 'Einsteinian world-view', since it was with Einstein's early work in relativity and quantum theory that the decisive change to a new basic notion of order set in. Already deep in the nineteenth century, especially with Faraday and Maxwell, there was a growing realization that to understand the nature of the universe a rather different concept of order was needed to replace that of a necessary and mechanical order. Investigation into the properties of electromagnetic induction revealed that the idea of instantaneous action at a distance is untenable, and called for a new idea of material substances as convergent points of force rather than as discrete corpuscles in empty space and time; while the discovery that all forces such as electricity, magnetism, and light are interrelated called correspondingly for a new theory of the world as a complex field of forces within which all movement and change involves time. It was left to Clerk Maxwell to provide mathematical clarification and interpretation of these insights, to develop a unified theory of electricity, magnetism, and light, and to come up with the laws of the field. However, Maxwell's acceptance of the notion of ether (which Faraday had rejected) created problems, for it meant that he had to retain a mechanical interpretation of the force field, and called in question Faraday's identification of matter and field. Out of this came Maxwell's famous partial differential equations for the electromagnetic field, which have been so outstandingly fertile for subsequent scientific discovery and advance.[17] At the same time Maxwell attempted a different type of field interpretation, not dependent on Newtonian mechanism, which while operating with matter and field as separated realities nevertheless held that in some way they interpenetrate one another.[18] Thus Faraday and Maxwell opened the way for a new understanding of nature in terms of field theory which could be set against the Newtonian outlook and which, in spite of Maxwell's acceptance of Newtonian dualism and mechanism, pointed to a non-mechanical view of the universe in which matter and field are unified.

The decisive step in this direction was taken by Einstein in his rejection of Newtonian dualism and mechanism. Following on clarification particularly by H. Hertz and H.A. Lorentz of difficult problems resulting from contradictions between Maxwellian and Newtonian mechanics, Einstein introduced a fundamental change into field theory, coordinating it with a startlingly new view of the universe and its unitary dynamic order, very different from the Newtonian world-view. He dethroned time and space from their absolute, unvarying, prescriptive role in the Newtonian system and brought them down to empirical reality, where he found them indissolubly integrated with its on-going processes. At the same time he set aside the idea of instantaneous action at a distance, but also set aside the existence of ether (still maintained by Lorentz) and all idea of the substantiality of the field (in Faraday's sense). There now emerged the concept of the continuous field of space–time which interacts with the constituent matter/energy of the universe, integrating everything within it in accordance with its unitary yet variable objective rational order of non-causal connections. Thus instead of explaining the behaviour of the field and all events within it in terms of the motion of separated material substances characterized by unique unchanging patterns and defined by reference to the conditioning of an inertial system, and therefore in terms of quantifiable motion and strict mechanical causes, Einstein explained it in terms of the objective configuration of the indivisible field and the dynamic invariant relatedness inherent in it—that is to say, in terms of the principle of relativity. It was the radical break with Newtonian mechanics and the Newtonian world-view that made relativity so difficult to grasp, but it was in coherence with this new understanding of the universe and its intrinsic order that Einstein also sought to develop quantum theory, without a duality of particle and field, which, as he believed, calls for the determination of relativistic field-structures in a proper scientific description of empirical reality, rather than a merely statistical account of quantum-experimental events and conditions. If a statistical approach is required in quantum mechanics it cannot rest content with offering an account of how experiments operate, but must offer an account of reality itself. All this implied the unification of matter and field in a dynamic, unbroken continuum—i.e. without the *contiguous* yet *discontinuous* connection of particles as in the Cartesian 'field'—which prompted Einstein to devote so much attention to developing a unified field theory and thereby determining the general laws of the whole indivisible field.[19] Although Einstein himself was not able to achieve this specific aim, nevertheless he succeeded, particularly through general relativity, as the staggering unfolding of its implications and the verification of its predictions have since shown, in opening the way toward a unified view of the universe with a very different conception of order.

The revolution in cosmology which all this entails represents a complete inversion in the Newtonian picture. For Newton the empirical world of phenomena characterized by relative apparent time and space was overarched by an unchanging infinite framework of absolute mathematical time and space which, while detached from empirical reality in that it remains completely unaffected by it at any point, causally conditions it throughout so that it is imprisoned within a rigid geometrical structure of a Euclidean sort. Here we have in effect a vast cosmological synthesis of the immutable God and the created universe. Such a universe is both infinite in its coordination with God and closed in upon its immanent necessities, which finally leaves no room for contingence or freedom. For Einstein, however, all that is as it were turned upside down. The controlling concept of the space-time metrical field implies the integration of finite space and time with physical reality, with the result that the universe may be described as 'finite and unbounded'. That is, so to say, instead of being closed from above down, the universe is to be regarded as open from below upward. The finite universe certainly has frontiers, but they are not frontiers at which it is turned back to be imprisoned in itself so much as frontiers where it is open indefinitely to what is beyond. Hence the finite universe cannot be what it actually is even as finite without being relativized by what transcends it. This may be expressed otherwise, in a more Einsteinian way. Instead of empirical reality being construed in terms of absolutely certain mathematical propositions clamped down upon it, which would inevitably introduce both rigidity and infinity into physics, mathematics is to be understood from its ground in objective, empirical structures of space–time, without distorting idealization which would make it irrelevant to experience. Thus it is through open mathematical structures appropriate to its nature that the universe really discloses to us the secrets of its latent order, which is of an open, contingent kind, with variables and spontaneities which we are unable to constrain and confine within our abstractive, logicist, and mechanist patterns of thought. Such an integration of the empirical and the mathematical in our interpretation of the universe allows its immanent rationalities to articulate and resonate in such a way that they point naturally and freely beyond their finite conditions and limits without being obstructed through artificial foreclosure on our part. In this event natural laws, in terms of which science seeks to describe the orderly behaviour of reality, may be formulated under conditions of the contingence of the universe, and thus without being cut off from the contingent basis upon which natural science rests, which would be the case if they were converted into necessary timeless truths of reason. As such, of course, natural laws are essentially and always open to revision in the light of what the universe may yet reveal of itself to our inquiries, for if they are true they are implicated in a dimension of rationality ranging indefinitely beyond them, and therefore must refer to much more than can be expressed in explicit terms at any time.

It must be pointed out that these two different world-views, the Newtonian and the Einsteinian, and the different kinds of order they entail, are not to be thought of as merely contradictory to one another.[20] There are certainly contradictions between a closed mechanist and determinist conception of the universe and an open-structured and non-determinist conception of it, but the reconstruction of the Newtonian outlook which we have to carry out on the basis of the Einsteinian outlook deduces the Newtonian as a limiting case of the Einsteinian on a lower level of scientific interaction with nature, much as classical physics is to be regarded as a limiting case of relativistic physics. That is to say, the Newtonian model of the universe cannot after all be regarded as a complete, self-contained, and self-explaining system, for if it is consistent as a scientific model it can be justified only by being completed beyond itself through coordination to a model characterized by a profounder and more comprehensive system of rational order. Thus the Newtonian model requires relation to the Einsteinian model if it is to retain any validity on its own limited basis.

A primary ingredient in this new Einsteinian model, which helps to give it a radically different character, is *time*, not time as an external geometric parameter as in the Newtonian model, but time as inherent in the empirical processes of physical reality, which demands that even inanimate matter must be considered as a dynamic and temporal state of affairs. However, with the introduction of time as an integral factor into our understanding and interpretation of the universe, we are no longer able, like the later Newtonians, to exclude from the spectrum of scientific inquiry all questions as to whence and whither, thereby restricting natural science artificially to questions as to what and how. That is to say,

questions about ultimate origins and ultimate ends must be
entertained by scientific inquiry, and also, more significantly,
the question why there is a universe at all rather than nothing
—if only because such questions help to open up to view the
distinctive nature of the universe. They have the effect, of
course, of considerably reinforcing the recovery of genuine
contingence in our grasp of the rational order in nature.
Here, then, we have an approach to the universe as a finite
yet continuous and unified whole which is to be interpreted
in terms of unbroken rational continuities rather than patterns
of static causality—i.e. in terms of reasons rather than causes.
All this is not to say that natural science through the properly
autonomous modes of inquiry which it develops can itself
answer questions about origins and ends, which in rigorous
fidelity to the nature of its empirical and contingent subject-
matter it must raise, but only that it should pursue its natural
investigations in such a way as to recognize these further
questions as rationally continuous and consistent with the
questions which it normally raises. Of course, if natural
science claimed that it could come up with answers to
those questions, in actuality it would thereby only shut the
door that they apparently open for us. It should be added,
however, that this would apply to all acts of the finite
reason which cannot of itself transcend its own finite limits
or therefore penetrate into ultimate origins or ends beyond
them. As the finite reason approaches these limits it is
thrown into a critical condition in which normal processes
of thought break down, for it is constrained both to entertain
the idea of a beginning and an end and yet to refrain from
entertaining it, but may nevertheless retain rational integrity
by postulating interaction with a rational movement from
beyond itself.

In accordance with its own nature, then, this new understanding of the universe, opened out for us through the
Einsteinian model, demands to be considered as a limiting
case of a still profounder and more comprehensive realm of
rational order. This is not to imply that the relation between
this and the Einsteinian system is precisely similar to that
between the Einsteinian and the Newtonian, for the different
conceptions of order entailed would introduce real dissimi-
larities into the cross-level connections, but only that this

Einsteinian type of order, particularly as it embraces contingence in such a profound way, requires relation to an order of rationality transcending it, if it is to retain rational integrity at its own natural level. The kind of relation envisaged here may perhaps be indicated by borrowing language from David Bohm as to the intersection of 'explicate' and 'implicate' orders,[21] for the kind of open contingent order disclosed in this new understanding of the universe is evidently implicated invisibly in a higher level of order beyond space and time as its ground, which cannot be articulated reductively in terms of the manifest explicate patterns of the lower level of order of space and time. Of course, the kind of ultimate intelligible ground with which theology is concerned is infinitely beyond any visible implicate order with which we may be concerned in physics.

We have now returned to the twofold orientation of contingent order, which we described theologically as contingence away from God and contingence toward God: contingence away from God toward an independent state of affairs in the created universe, and contingence toward God as the creative ground and reason for the unitary rational order and relative autonomy of the universe. The deeply based intersection between these two approaches, and the two world-views to which they give rise, does not involve anything like a cosmological synthesis of the Creator and the contingent order. Nor does it involve the development of a specific theological cosmology of the kind which could be held in a one-to-one correspondence with the coordinates of a natural scientific cosmology, or even in a partial differential relation to it. Full justice must be done to contingence on both sides of the intersecting relation: the free contingent activity of God in creating the universe out of nothing and ceaselessly sustaining it in being, and the free contingent existence of the universe with a rational order of its own by divinely given creaturely right. How are we, then, to spell out what is involved or at least required of us in the two-fronted orientation of contingent order?

1. The fact that the universe, as we understand it in theology, is coordinated to the unlimited rationality and freedom of God the Creator, implies that it has a freedom and flexibility in its order which makes it capable of a variety of consistent

interpretations and cognate cosmological formalizations. Theology can make no specific contribution to the development of any such cosmology: that belongs to the purview and freedom of natural science. Because the universe is God's creation, theological science cannot but be deeply interested in the uncovering through natural scientific inquiry of the rational patterns which God has conferred upon it, if only in Christian concern for praise and worship of the Creator by the creation.

2. The fact that both theological science and natural science have a stake in the contingence of the universe and its order implies that the intersection between their different world-views has to do with basic forms of rationality in the space-time universe in which each shares in its own distinctive way. This gives theology no ground for standing aloof from the cosmological discoveries made by natural science, but rather ground for seeking fuller understanding of their rational basis in the space-time universe, within which theology also must develop adequate accounts of its own convictions about incarnation and resurrection, for example, as well as creation, with proper respect for their empirical correlates in the spatio-temporal structures of empirical reality. Yet theology can do this only as at the same time it clarifies for science as well as for itself the transcendent relation of the Creator to what he has made and continues to uphold through his sustaining power and rationality.

3. Since the new scientific view of the universe is not hostile to the Christian faith, theology has no need to be on the defensive as it often felt it had to be when confronted with the dualist and determinist conception of the universe as a closed continuum of cause and effect, which axiomatically ruled out of consideration any real notion of God's providential interaction with the world or therefore of prayer, not to mention notions of incarnation and redemption. Rather is it now possible for theology to engage in constructive dialogue with natural science, not only for its own good but for the good of science also. Dialogue can help theology to purify its apparatus of concept and term from time-conditioned and pseudo-theological as well as pseudo-scientific lumber, freeing it to unfold knowledge of the living God on the proper ground of his self-revelation to mankind within the

structured objectivities and intelligibilities of the space–time world where God has placed them. Dialogue can also help natural science, in view of its recurring temptation to resolve contingence away, to remain faithful to the nature of created or contingent reality, upon the recognition of which its empirico-theoretical activity is based, and therefore to remain open to the realization that the universe is what it is as a whole because of its implication in a transcendent rational order, in God.

4

Contingence and Disorder

i. From Contingence to Necessity

Throughout the history of thought, pre-Christian and post-Christian, contingence has regularly been contrasted with necessity, for contingent things do not have to be and contingent events do not have to happen. They can be and not be, but once they are, they are what they are in dependence on something else which is not itself contingent. However, contingence has been variously understood in accordance with the nature of that on which contingent things and events depend and on the way in which they depend on it, so that differences have arisen as to how far they are open to scientific investigation and interpretation. In classical Greek thought, whether of a Platonic or an Aristotelian kind, rational knowledge was held to be possible only of things and events which cannot but be what they are in their causes, i.e. where necessary (logical or causal) relations obtain. Hence contingent things and events which are particular, changeable, and uncertain and which subsist only accidentally, were held to be not properly knowable for they could not be construed in terms of necessary and universal connections or determinate forms. Since the contingent has to do with matter rather than form which gives matter its actual existence, it was regarded as indeterminate and deficient in form, with only an accidental relation to being, and therefore as deficient in reality and rationality: it was a kind of non-being. In such a general outlook it is understandable that with radically dualist positions, in which matter and form, the sensible and the intelligible, were sharply contrasted, the contingent should be connected with indeterminacy, disorder, and evil, for it represented a privation of order and being. It was with that idea, deeply entrenched in Graeco-Roman culture, that Christianity had to struggle, not only in its bizarre forms in Manichaeism and

Gnosticism, but in its attractive Neoplatonic form. And it was out of that struggle that Christian theology produced its radicalized concept of the contingence and intrinsic rationality of all created reality, which has left an ineradicable mark on all Western science.

Basically the same problems persisted, however, in Western mediaeval thought, in spite of the revolutionary work of Greek patristic theology and science, for Neoplatonic and Aristotelian thought staged a powerful resurgence in the Augustinian and Thomist developments. The classical model of science, according to which the object of scientific investigation must be necessary and universal — everything incidental or accidental being excluded from the possibility of genuine knowledge — was generally followed and accepted, together with the Aristotelian way of relating matter, form and causality. On the other hand, the Christian conception of creation, in accordance with which all creaturely beings are such that they would be non-beings if left to themselves, introduced modification into the Aristotelian system which affected the notion of contingence.[1] While contingence continued to be defined by reference of effect to cause, the nature of the Supreme Cause, God the Creator, was differently regarded, as was also the way in which contingent things and events depend on him. In creating and sustaining the world, and in imposing upon it an all-embracing divine order, God was held to provide necessary causes for effects which he willed to be necessary; but for effects which he willed to be free God was also held to provide what St. Thomas Aquinas called 'contingent active causes', i.e. causes which are able to act otherwise.[2] Thus contingent things and events were considered to be related to their cause in such a way that they could be and not be from it. Of course, it was argued, if all things in the world were contingent (that is, might not have been at all) nothing would ever have begun to be, for nothing begins to be except because of something that is — a being whose existence is necessary or one which must exist by its very nature. If such a necessary and primary reality were to disappear, nothing would remain. Every effect in the world, therefore, must be understood to depend ultimately on God as the First Cause who transcends and (as the Unmoved Mover) inertially determines the whole cosmic order. So far as contingence is concerned, this means that in the last analysis contingent things and events obtain only under condition of extrinsic relation to what is necessary.[3] Taken in conjunction with the scientific model noted above, which stands for the dominance of the universal over the particular, the essential over the accidental, and the necessary over the contingent, this had the effect of resolving contingence away in the claim that no scientific knowledge of contingent things and events is possible in so far as they are contingent. All that may be done is to illumine them in the whole system of things in the world with some form of rationality which they do not have of themselves.[4] Regarded in themselves, contingent things and events appear to be quite baffling and elusive, for they have no independence or enduring self-identity of their own. They are separated particulars or singularities which defy rational knowledge and which are capable of being construed in rational discourse only indirectly through being subsumed into relation with a series of necessary reasons.

This way of rationalizing contingence exerted such power that, even in the later Middle Ages when there was a growing tendency toward empirical realism, singularities and concrete connections apprehended in actual existence were resolved into abstractive forms capable of being handled by the accepted model of science. Thus images and concepts signifying and describing contingent things and events were transposed into second-order terms which stood for but did not directly refer to them (that is, into linguistic and logical facts), which have their meaning in syntactical complexes and propositional sequences and which are capable through logical and necessary argumentation of demonstrating universal truths. Hence any promise held out by late mediaeval developments of a genuinely empirical science that could take contingence seriously as having an intelligibility of its own (an idea that derived from Duns Scotus),[5] was undercut by a highly formal conception of science which overcame and transmuted contingence, for it operated finally only with propositions, and indeed with necessary propositions in a syntactic or logico-deductive system which have no more than an oblique bearing upon objective reality.[6]

Within this general outlook contingence and disorder would

seem not to be unconnected, for in so far as contingent things and events are contingent they are accidental or deficient in necessity and therefore lack both being and order. Just as contingent things and events depend on what is itself not contingent, so disorder has no autonomous existence of its own but obtains only as it depends on the order from which it detracts: it is to be understood only privatively, as the impairment or perversion of order. This would allow for an accidental but not a substantial role for physical evil in the universe. No evil could ever have a reality of its own, for nothing essentially evil could exist: rather is it a sort of non-being, parasitic upon being, which corrupts and distorts its natural form and order and thereby withdraws from being.[7] While it partakes of what is subject to change and corruption, physical evil obtains as the failure of something to reach its due form or appropriate end, for example, in the birth of a monster. Clearly this would apply only to particular things and events or to some partial order of secondary causes, and not to the general order of the world which, as it derives from and depends on God himself, is essentially good and without imperfection or disorder. So far as particular cases are concerned, evil is to be understood as an imperfection, as an incidental not-yet in the process of becoming, as an accidental failure in fulfilment, or as a mischance when the fortuitous reception of a partial form involves the loss of a proper form.[8] The principle of imperfection or physical evil, however, is not to be found in the form of things and events, for form is the principle of order and determinate being, but in the matter of indeterminate substratum of things and events, which has no autonomous existence but is the medium between non-being and being. Hence the further down the ladder of being matter-bound things and events are, and the less implicated they are in form, the more they have within them the possibility of indeterminacy and disorder. Matter, as Aristotle claimed, resists form. It would seem, then, on this view that ultimately it is the recalcitrance of matter, or sheer passive facticity, which is the disturber of order in the universe.[9]

On the other hand, as St. Thomas argued, since evil is always only a deficiency of the good and always dependent on it, it is to goodness itself that one must look for anything like its 'material cause'.[10] Out of his goodness God created the universe in its matter as well as its form to be good. Hence we must think of God as permitting physical evil to have its place in the universe in order to contribute to its order and perfection, not of itself but accidentally, that is, in such a way that under his providential overruling it serves the synthesis of differences in all parts of the universe, and the good collective arrangement of the universe as a whole. Indeed, if in the world as we know it, which is an order of becoming involving coming into being and ceasing to be—or life and death (the lion must eat and the kid be killed) – all evil were taken away, much good would disappear with it. There must be physical evil in the universe, St. Thomas claimed, if it is to be ordered and structured in the harmonious way it is. God's care in creating and preserving all things is to bring good out of evils, not just to abolish them, and to bring everything throughout the whole range of existence from the lowest to the highest level of created being to its true form and order, with nothing left defective or imperfect.[11]

It is highly significant that while this way of thinking out the question of evil in the universe acknowledges evil in natural things and conditions, it treats evil as an absence of natural form or order, and thereby precludes the notion of a *natural* evil as it does of a *natural* disorder. Evil and disorder wherever they occur are always unnatural.[12] Hence one must think only in terms of natural order, or natural law, which is the expression of divine order in the universe, and of physical evil wherever it occurs in nature only as a privation and not as an antithesis to that order. Such a view of evil has its distinct advantages. It does recognize the hard fact of physical evil or disorder in nature—disaster, calamity, suffering, disease, etc.—and yet it denies that evil as such enters into the orderly establishment of created reality or belongs to the perfection of the universe, for while evil admittedly contributes to its order and perfection, it does so only indirectly by reason of its incidental conjunction with what is good.

Here we have ruled out of consideration any idea that evil has a direct cause (such as a formal or final cause, to use Aristotelian terminology), which would imply that evil must be traced back to a source in God—although the admission cannot be avoided that God permits evil, and even wills structures and events in the universe which result in physcial affliction and disorder, such as earthquakes. There is also ruled out of consideration any idea that evil is a principle in itself with its own operative reasons, which would imply the impossible notion of an ultimate dualism of good and evil, with two realms equally poised in being and power in opposition to one another. On the other hand, while mediaeval thought certainly rejected the idea that God is in any way, even indirectly, responsible for moral evil (for it is repugnant to his nature), the question must be raised whether it took the terrible reality of physical evils in the universe seriously enough, for are they not also repugnant to the nature of God? Should we not raise the question as to radical evil, evil not just as privation but as negation, that is, as a positively disordering factor in the universe? If so, this would certainly make the problem of evil much more difficult, yet that is no reason for not facing up to what it actually is.

Moreover, the idea that goodness in some indirect way 'causes' evil by providing the ground on which evil subsists and disorder arises, is one thing when evil is construed in a merely privative or negative way; but it is a very different thing if evil is something more than that, for then evil must be thought of as using goodness for a malevolent end. This is something with which we are only too familiar in the modern world, as terrorists so often justify their evil acts by reference to the requirements and structures of justice itself, but by latching on to justice and manipulating its claims upon us for their own ends, they only compound the malevolence of their evil acts. Thus so far as moral evil is concerned we encounter again and again in human society a strange moral perversion which, as Polanyi has so often pointed out, feeds upon a moral perfectionism and gives rise to fearfully wicked acts.[13] However, is there any evidence for a malignant twist in the physical order of the universe, a malevolence in nature itself?

Further, if evil is no more than a privation of the good or a defection in order, is it ultimately anything more than a form of what ancient and mediaeval thought generally called 'contingent' or 'accidental' being, and indeed a sort of non-being, which is overcome in the reception of form and the actualization of true being, and which, therefore, in our understanding of it may be resolved away by rational forms of thought? Does not that way of linking evil or disorder with contingence imply a very one-sided and distorted notion of contingence as well as of disorder? Certainly it does not allow for any notion that contingent realities may have an independence and an objective order or intelligibility of their own, for by definition contingence is deficient in being and order and thereby open to the possibility of disorder—left to themselves contingent things and events can only retreat from order and being into chaos and non-being. However, when contingence is realized to imply both independence and dependence and is radicalized to refer not simply to singularities or separated particulars in the universe but to the distinctive nature and order of all created reality, do we not need to rethink the whole question of disorder or physical evil?

These questions are still very much with us, for throughout the developments of modern thought and science since mediaeval times the same basic idea has persisted that contingence obtains only under conditions of necessity, or—to express it otherwise—the contingent is to be understood not in terms of mere chance but as a form of the necessary under a condition.[14] As such, contingence is and must be overcome in the drive of the scientific reason to identify and formalize necessary features in nature, but there have been variations upon this general theme, for the balance of emphasis upon the contingent and upon the necessary has not always been the same.

A vast switch in outlook took place during the Renaissance and the Reformation which differentiates modern from mediaeval thought. With the Renaissance there took place a rediscovery of the diversity of nature and of man's integration with nature, and with the Reformation there arose a deeper respect for the created order of nature and a recovery of the early Christian understanding of contingence and contingent intelligibility.[15] The combination of both of these gave rise to empirical science as we know it, but the old problematic remained and became even more acute. This was largely due to the carry-over of habits of thought from classical culture, which was reinforced by the Enlightenment as well as the Renaissance, together with the great new emphasis, so closely associated with Galileo, upon the quantification of all observed phenomena and experimental data.[16] Thus developed, natural science was concerned, not so much with a description of the nature of things in themselves, in their 'hidden causes'—to a certain extent this represents a revulsion from Aristotle—but with a mathematical organization of experimental results through deductive geometrical models. This had the effect of imposing upon scientific inquiry into phenomenal and empirical processes a way of thinking about them within a frame of ideal conditions, and that in turn gave rise to idealized patterns in the formulation of scientific knowledge in which contingent features and relations in the actual world were rationalized away. The general trend was set by Descartes, Newton, and Leibniz, who in different ways developed scientific methods of determining regularities discovered in nature and of formalizing them into necessary universal laws. The movement of thought was steadily from contingence to necessity, or rather from apparent contingence to underlying necessity, which was given a massive deterministic form through Kant's transposition of causality from the objective connections which things have externally with one another in the world into a regulative and necessary principle of scientific thought. Yet this implied a constructivist concept of scientific knowledge which carried it beyond Kant's own intention into the positivism of Ernst Mach and his followers.[17]

With Mach this necessitarian line of thought crosses another that began from the other side of the dualism between the phenomenal and geometrical aspects of nature stemming from Galileo. In this development emphasis was laid upon actual experience of the properties of nature, upon the irreducible particularity and stubborn factuality of phenomena, which demand a natural, empirical interpretation —in reaction to any approach which clamped down upon nature absolute mathematical structures of a transcendental sort, and therefore in rejection of any claim to be able to determine necessary and immutable laws inherent in nature. On this view, then, the concern of natural science is simply with the discovery of natural laws which describe how as a matter of fact things and events take place in the world of our experience, not with how they have to be or have to take place, nor is natural science by implication concerned with things and events as if they might not have been or might have been otherwise—for no considerations beyond what is actually there are allowed. Here apparently a form of contingence, limited by immediate experience, as undiluted natural facticity, comes back, but it represents at the same time an empiricist revolt against the mediaeval stress upon the natural order and the Reformation stress upon the created order of things in the world. That is to say, it is a notion of contingence without any dependence on necessity to lend it rationality, and yet without any independent rationality of its own in virtue of which it may be apprehended. Here the old antithesis between chance and necessity disappears, for they are ultimately one and the same in what happens to be there: they merge in a brute factual necessity.[18]

It was with David Hume that this empiricist line of thought was given its classical, and most consistent, expression: through his claim that we have no knowledge except what comes to us through the senses, and consequently through his questioning of any observable necessity or causal nexus between events in nature and therefore of any objective order in created or natural reality.[19] That is not to deny belief in necessity or causality, for the world is what it is and cannot be otherwise, so that belief in necessity or causality is 'causally conditioned' in us—not evidentially or logically conditioned in us, for we have no immediate experience of it and can have no demonstrative knowledge of it.[20] When we ask what this means, Hume offers a genetic or naturalistic account of it. The conjunction between events with which we operate in our thought derives from 'a determination of the mind' which has taken root in us because it has proved practically convenient in our interaction with the world around us and the sequences we experience in it.[21] That is to say, Hume offered a distinctly psychological and pragmatic account of knowledge, ordinary and scientific, but it is a strange kind of 'knowledge', for strictly speaking it entails no cognitively valid claims about objective reality beyond sense experience, but can operate only with judgements of belief and convenience grounded in the constitution of human nature. In this event the traditional antithesis between order and disorder could have no basis in empirical experience, for order and disorder could only be what human beings, individually and socially, make of relation to the world as it actually is in its phenomenal relation to them. That would undercut, however, Hume's own argument that disorder in the world counts against belief in God which tacitly presumes that there is an objective order in nature.[22] Quite evidently there are inherent contradictions and self-destructive elements in a consistently empiricist position.

As the empiricist, positivist, and naturalistic line of thought developed from Hume into the next two centuries it was certainly found difficult to maintain a purely pragmatic view of science in face of the astonishing march of discovery and its operationally valid conceptions about the nature of the physical universe. Thus some concession to the claim that scientific knowledge is subject to the constraints of objective reality could hardly be avoided, if only in a grudging admission that scientific concepts and statements might be related to objective reality in some oblique manner, yet only in such a way that nothing more may be 'established' than relative and constantly revisable 'truth'; relative and revisable, that is, not in any correspondence with alleged intrinsic structures in external reality, but in congruence with the operational success of instrumental control of experience and the most convenient and economic arrangements of observational data that can be achieved at the time. The real problem at the heart of this development, however, was its in-built constructivism—the idea that the human reason, as Hume once expressed it, even in demonstrative sciences must be considered as 'a kind of cause of which truth is the natural effect'.[23] While that took a synthetic *a priori* form in Kant's reconstruction of the epistemological basis of natural science, here it took a naturalistic form derived from the inner constitutive adaptation of human behaviour in physico-biological continuity with the evolution of nature. Thus Ernst Mach regarded everyday thinking and science in general 'as a biological and organic phenomenon, in which logical thinking assumed the position of an ideal limiting case'.[24] The only kind of scientific conceptions allowed on this view were those grounded in basic ideas empirically and pragmatically acquired through trial and error acheivements which have been assimilated into the human and social behaviour of the race. That is to say, the world-as-we-come-to-know-it through scientific investigation, description, and organization is what man has formed for himself in creative interaction with his environment—any notion of an ontological order beyond sense perception or experience is denigrated as deriving from imagination, religion, or metaphysics. The paradox is that this position comprises a narrow rationalistic metaphysics of a positivist and empiricist sort which is all the more dogmatic because it is tacitly assumed and is not opened to questioning!

Feeding into this line of development, while being itself deeply influenced by it, was the persistent idea that science proceeds by way of abstraction and deduction from observations, which had the effect of reinforcing and widening the dualism inherent in post-Galilean science between appearance and reality, or subject and object, so that there took place a transposition of emphasis from the context of objects or realities perceived to the context of sense impressions or immediate awareness of them in the human consciousness, for it is only upon the certainty we have of the latter, it was claimed, that scientific knowledge can be built. This switch from the objective to the subjective pole of knowledge, however, led to the displacement of the basic intention of science—to understand reality—by another that was radically man-centred and instrumentalist.

It is important to note that this movement of thought involved both a detachment from ontological reality and a flight into conventionalism and logicism. Instead of operating with a realist understanding of 'facts' as they are forced on us by hard empirico-theoretical evidence and with fact-orientated scientific conceptions and statements, empiricist and positivist science now operated with abstractions from sense experience logically elaborated and defined, that is, with logical constructs out of sensations. Since these constructs arose out of abstractive procedures detaching phenomenal sense-data from their alleged ground in objective or external reality, they have to be handled by science apart from any ontological reference beyond themselves, and therefore with an intentional 'non-actuality' and 'non-evidence (reminding us of Ockham's 'intentional inexistence'). As such they are represented in thought by symbolic conventions—'thought-symbols' as Mach called them[25] which have only an analytic character and are capable of being organized into necessary and compelling logico-deductive systems. Regarded from this point of view, scientific theories are logically tautological and can have no claim to bear upon intrinsic relations or structures in being, while scientific laws are devoid of evidential content and are finally no more than freely created sets of conventions for the most effective and economic organization of observational and operational data, yet they are not altogether arbitrary sets of conventions for they have to be consistent with one another.

Thus it turns out that the empiricist line of development in modern science, which sought to ground all knowledge exclusively on immediate experience in renunciation of any attempt to establish necessary connections in observable empirical regularities, ends up by taking refuge in self-sufficient logically necessary connections between propositions. Here the traditional distinction between contingency and necessity which referred to different states of affairs in the world of being, yields place to one which refers to different kinds of statement, for contingent statements about scientific data (concrete empirical descriptions of matters of fact) are resolved through logical reinterpretation and generalization into necessary statements held to be universally valid and not to need experimental justification. We are reminded of the point at which the late mediaeval emphasis on empirical realism ended up, as Ockhamistic nominalism passed into terminism in its substitution of syntactical and logical relations for real and actual relations. One is reminded also of the thought of Quine in our own day who resolves singular terms by transposing them from a semantic to a syntactical context where they are logically redefined and may be deployed significantly without onto-logical reference to entities beyond them.[26]

The translation of scientific processes of thought into contingent and necessary propositions, however, need not be without value, if they are rescued from the morass of nominalistic tautologies. No set of necessary propositions can be regarded as complete in itself, as if the set could generate its own proof, for the definitions of the basic propositions or axioms in the set cannot but rely upon undefined and unexplained assumptions which, so far as the set of necessary propositions is concerned, are logically contingent. That is to say, if we translate this back into the context of empirical reality, no generalization of scientific theories into natural laws can eradicate contingent features from our knowledge of the universe without being rendered empty and meaningless. Thus in so far as they are consistent and valid, scientific theories and laws repose upon contingent factors which cannot be bracketed out of their equations even though they make them incomplete. Hence even if we identify contingence with singularity in the narrower sense of stubborn particularity or individuality, we find that, far from having to be explained away, contingence retains a highly significant place in the universe as we explore and seek to map it. In this event, contingence cannot be treated as a disordering factor in the universe, but rather as an all-important ingredient making for the astonishing richness and variability of nature, which constantly defies our capacity to anticipate it or to reduce it to our standardizing formalizations. Indeed it is precisely because we find ourselves having to reckon with this ingredient that we are convinced that our scientific theories are locked into reality.

ii. From Necessity to Contingence

We have been considering the movement of empirical scientific thought in its double form as it took off from Galilean dualism in which an experimental approach to nature, coordinated with a quantifying interpretation of phenomena, set the pattern of development, and have seen that it can be regarded as a variegated but steady argument from contingence to necessity, involving persistent abstraction from empirical and contingent states of affairs. We have given disproportionate attention to the course of positivist science, since it has come to exercise such a potent influence not only on modern philosophy and the human and social sciences but upon the general climate of opinion. There is much more to this story, however, which we cannot recapitulate here, especially on the non-positivist line of development which has to do with the great transition of realist science from classical physics through Maxwellian physics to relativistic physics. Here we have a growing, if reluctant, realization against traditional scientific habits of mind that there are serious discrepancies between classical (idealizing) mathematicization and the dynamic nature of empirical reality, particularly evident in the way in which the mechanistic approach to nature was being undermined and shown to be inadequate, and indeed artificial. It was slowly coming to be seen that there is a stubborn, resistant contingence about nature which cannot be reduced just to contingent features in the universe, singularities which are ultimately irreducible to explanatory models of thought, but which is a universal property of the universe in its parts and as a whole, and of the nature of its order. Nothing short of a radical reconstruction of the relation of scientific theory to this distinctive nature of empirical reality was needed if science was really to cope with it in a more adequate way. The basic problem, as E.L. Mascall has pointed out, can be traced back to 'the ultimate inability of Galilean and Newtonian physics to coordinate the observational and experimental facts.'[27] It was at that point, therefore, that the revolution had to bite most deeply when it came—and it did, with the destruction of the Kantian and Machian idea that we are unable to know things in themselves, and with the advent of relativity and quantum physics. It will be sufficient to indicate briefly the profound import of these changes as they bear upon our theme.

1. So long as it was held that we cannot know things in their internal relations, it was possible to treat atoms, or light particles, for example, as scientific fictions to which there were no corresponding entities in nature, mere 'thought-symbols' which we can conveniently manipulate for our own pragmatic ends in interaction with nature; and it was also possible to operate with the assumption that the kind of necessities we develop in our mathematical formalizations correspond to a similar necessity inherent in nature—for there could be no objective test or control of these assumptions, apart from second-order criteria such as operational success or convenience in economical representation. Mach's conception of the atom as no more than a 'mental artifice' and of atomic theory as only 'a mathematical *model* for facilitating the mental reproduction of facts', is a case in point.[28] But when physics succeeded in penetrating into the

internal structure of the atom and establishing some knowledge of its internal relations, he had to give up his objection to the reality of atoms.[29] Thus the sheer success of atomic physics called for a new realism in science which required a profounder integration of experiment and theory than the positivists allowed. What was required was a cross-level coordination between sets of mathematical relations and sets of contingent relations, without reading the specific kind of order that obtains in one into the other—that is, without confusing mathematical structures with ontic structures, while acknowledging the constraint of ontic structures on mathematical formalization. It is this more realist way of bringing together theoretical structures with empirical correlates without imposing idealized or necessitarian models upon them, that has been having such a profound effect in natural science, for its spells the end of a tyrannical scientism, and liberates the natural coherences and patterns latent in the world so that they may be understood and interpreted in accordance with their own contingent orderliness unhindered by artificial abstraction.[30] Moreover, taken together with the concept of order forced on us by relativity and quantum physics, this deeper realism disposes of the old Humean argument that if we could penetrate into the inner nature of things we would find that they were governed by necessity, that they could not be otherwise.

2. The classical notion of connection between events assumed a rigid framework of thought in accordance with which nature was regarded as divided up into separated and unalterable particles which act only externally on one another at definite localities in space and time—in abstraction from the natural cohesions which contingent realities and events may already have.[31] This made it possible with the aid of differential equations to offer an idealized mathematical account of causal connections, thereby importing into them an absolute mathematical necessity—which gave rise to the mechanist and determinist view of the universe. But all this is radically changed when nature is found not to be ultimately divided up like that but, all its particulate properties notwithstanding, is dynamically continuous in space and time, in such a way that all things are what they are through unbroken internal relations with other things, while those inter-relations help to

make them what they actually are or become. Here there is
no idealizing abstraction of phenomena from their natural
cohesions in the constituent matter and energy of the
universe, and even space and time are not split apart from one
another or regarded as divisible into discrete localities and
intervals. This four-dimensional continuous indivisible field of
space-time relations is far from being merely a scientific
'thought-symbol', for it constitutes the fundamental continuum of the universe in which energy and matter, field and
particle, form and being, are fully integrated, and as such provides the objective dynamic structure ordering all things and
events in the universe. That is what now takes the place of the
empty continuum in which energy and matter, field and
particle, form and being are not internally integrated, i.e. the
kind that comprises a series of separated contiguous things
or events externally bearing upon one another. Thus the idea
of force acting at a distance and across intervals of time,
with which classical causality was bound up, falls away, and
nature is understood in terms of its own contingent order.
The functioning of the space-time metrical field, realistically
conceived, with the interdependence of all its constituent
energy and matter, lies behind the rational patterns and
structures of the universe. Such is the vast change effected
by relativity physics: classical causal relations are replaced by
a dynamic inherent relatedness in the universe, in which
space and time are included within the internal connections
of all empirical realities and processes and are inseparable
from them as space-time. Mechanical laws are discarded
along with the rigid structure of classically defined space and
time, and field laws are formulated instead, which describe
the dynamic invariances of space-time as an orderly open
continuum of contingent realities and events.

3. Quantum physics has proved an even greater challenge to
the classical way of coordinating theoretical structure with
experimental results, for it has brought to light deep connections in nature which resist determinist or idealized forms
of thought, especially in respect of static (geometrically
defined) localities in space and time. That is to say, the
necessary theoretical relations and concepts which are
associated with the setting up of an experiment in accordance
with the principles of classical or Newtonian mechanics, are

in sharp conflict with the non-necessary or contingent relations and concepts forced on our thought by the behaviour of the quanta as it is disclosed through that experiment —that is, of course, when the two sets of relations and concepts are considered on one and the same logical level. The fact that the contingent relations cannot be transposed and reconstrued in terms of necessary relations gives no ground for denying that they may have a deeper rational order of their own not amenable to interpretation from a determinate (classical) frame of reference, or that the two levels in terms of which the different relations are defined may not be significantly correlated with one another. The basic problem, evidently, has to do with the fact that while one level operates with a duality of field and particle, which are elaborated into a necessary continuity entailing the classical conception of localities in space and time, the other deeper level implies an integration of field and particle which requires the abandonment of the classical notion of locality. Thus it is understandable that the contingent connections at the deeper level, which make for open or incomplete structures, when interpreted from a determinate frame of reference, should appear to be discontinuous, indeterminate, or uncertain. Clearly, if the experimental results (which are quite massive) are not to be violated, that determinate framework must be opened out and reconstructed through a relativistic integration of field and particle, so that the difficult problems of quantum change in time and place (which gave rise to the so-called 'uncertainty principle') may disappear, as the classical notion of causality is abandoned. In that event the theoretical structure might be correlated significantly with the contingent relations disclosed in the behaviour of the quanta, to bring to light their intrinsic order, when the old individual laws of elementary particles would be abandoned, not so much in favour of statistical laws governing aggregations and determining probabilities, as in favour of field laws (in Einstein's sense) describing the properties and interconnections of elementary particles in the force-field with which they are constitutively and inseparably bound up. As such these field laws would have to be open-structured and formally incomplete, for they must themselves be contingent in character if they are to be appropriate.

There is much here that is yet to be resolved, but whatever form quantum or particle theory may take in the future, quantum physics has already made it very clear that nature is characterized by profound contingent features having an integration of form and being which will not allow them to be categorized as irrational or disorderly. If they resist complete formalization they may nevertheless be illuminatingly coordinated with theoretical structures at other levels of scientific activity and conception in such a way as to bring to light and throw into relief their own subtle contingent orderliness. With such contingent relations and concepts incorporated into basic physical laws, the universe described by natural science through the unification of relativity and quantum theory cannot but manifest an openness in which its latent rational order points beyond itself.

This stratification of theoretical structure that has arisen in quantum physics is something that is increasingly being forced on scientific thought under the constraint of the intrinsic rationality of nature, i.e. not only in respect of the relation of sub-atomic to atomic levels, but of physico-chemical to biological levels, and of the biological to the human and social levels of intelligent existence. The universe thus appears as a multi-levelled and multi-variable complex of rational order in which the different levels are hierarchically coordinated with one another. Each level is subject to what Michael Polanyi has called 'the principle of marginal control', in accordance with which the organizational principles of one level govern those of a 'lower' level through its boundary conditions where it is left open or indeterminate, but it is itself controlled in a similar way from the level 'above' it.[32] From a purely theoretical point of view this seems to imply that we have to reckon with an indefinite number of levels all open 'upward' but not reducible 'downward', but in actual fact this is not the case, since the universe is finite: bounded by limits at the 'lowest' level (the zero-point of temperature or the quantum state of lowest energy) and at the 'highest' level (the finite speed of light) within which natural scientific activity is restrained. Regarded in this way the 'highest' level marks the limit of empirical reality where the universe as an intelligible system is left open at its boundary conditions to what is beyond it; but the 'lowest' level, with which we have to do in quantum or particle physics, while having boundary conditions at which it is left open to control from 'above' it, marks the limit of empirical reality in respect of its initial conditions or ultimate givenness, the irreducible contingent facticity, behind which or beneath which we are unable to probe, for there we are at the very edge of being where it is bounded by non-being or nothing. That is what makes the contingent order we are up against in quantum physics so baffling, for we cannot get our thought behind it, but must accept it for what it actually is in itself in its sheer givenness. Nevertheless it is what it is only within the whole intelligible system of the universe and thus requires to be coordinated with the level or levels 'above' it, for it needs to be completed beyond itself. It is what it becomes and becomes what it is, unfolding its inner rationality, as other levels interact with it and contribute to the fulness of its rational order at the boundary conditions where it is rationally left indeterminate for them and integrated with the whole system of rationality in the universe.

Far from being a defect, this indeterminate feature at the 'lowest' or quantum level of reality is essential to the dynamic structure of functioning of its contingent rational order. Since indeterminate contingent relations at that level require to interact with rational order beyond themselves in order to constitute the contingent rational order that they do, they cannot be regarded as ground for any disorder that may possibly arise, for any interference in their order could only come from 'above' them. In having come into being, contingent relations cannot but be what they are—they cannot be other than contingent or the ultimately given—and so may be said to have a 'contingent necessity' of their own which, of course, does not mean that they had to come into being or could not have been otherwise, and cannot therefore be confused with an absolute necessity. Regarded in this way the contingent order of the basic or quantum level of reality is the most stable and rational of all, while as providing the ground base for the whole structure of the multi-levelled universe it contributes an ineradicable openness to all the ontological and rational levels in the universe and to the universe as a whole, making it a stable open system.

Our consideration of the great switch in the outlook of

natural science, to which empirico-theoretical grasp of things in their internal relations and relativity theory and quantum theory have contributed so effectively, has shown us that the movement of thought from contingence to necessity has been halted, for it has entailed a revision of prevailing theoretical structures in science in order to eliminate from them idealized and closed necessitarian patterns of thought, and thus to make room for contingence. The spatial metaphor of 'below' and 'above' which we have been using, however, may conceal the far-reaching import of this change in the movement of thought. If we turn the multi-levelled structure of thought we have been considering the other way round—as in some respects would seem to be required by the coincidence of the quantum relations that obtain at the microphysical level with those that obtain at the astrophysical level—then we must think of necessitarian relations that arise through abstractive and idealizing operations as limiting cases of 'higher' levels of more open and flexible order, and as rationally requiring boundary conditions where they are left indeterminate or open for control by those 'higher' levels of more open and flexible order. From this perspective the movement of thought from contingence to necessity may be said not just to have been halted but actually to have been reversed. This does not imply any logical argument from necessity to contingence, which would be a contradiction in terms, but a movement of thought turning away from necessity to the acceptance of contingence in its own natural right and order. This would imply a readiness to accept the radicalized concept of contingence and contingent order that derives from the classical foundations of early Christian theology, which natural science in modern times has presupposed in its very foundations but which it has steadily obscured through its strange craving for necessity.

When this return to radical contingence is aligned to the empiricist movement of thought, however, it engenders a positivist phenomenalism or a positivist existentialism such as we find in the thought, respectively, of Maurice Merleau-Ponty or Jean Paul Sartre.[33] Behind both of these thinkers lies not so much the basic switch in scientific thought which we have been considering, as a philosophical revolt against the traditional and especially Thomist argument from contingence to God who through his necessary and timeless being inertially grounds and orders all empirical existence, thereby imparting to it a necessitation which undermines its distinctively contingent nature. With Sartre this takes the form of an impassioned atheistic existentialism, in the claim that belief in God is incompatible with the contingence of bodily existence and with the freedom of man, and that rejection of God is needed to save contingency and freedom. Only if God does not exist, he held, can there be beings whose existence comes before their essence, i.e. whose actual existence is free from any prior or objective order of necessity or meaning to constrain them.[34] If existence precedes essence, 'there is no determinism—man *is* free, man *is* freedom'.[35]

This rejection of God is admittedly embarrassing for the existentialist, for without God man is bereft of any intelligible or transcendent realm of values, and is thrown back upon himself as the creative source of value and meaning in the world.[36] Here we find the thought of Sartre linking up with the pragmatist and constructivist line of thought from Hume to Mach, for which there is no cause or effect in nature, for nature has only individual existence and simply is. For man, on Sartre's view, this means that his life is nothing (unrelieved contingence) until he lives it, and its value is nothing but the sense he chooses to make of it. He constantly makes himself through his choices, defines himself by his commitments and actions, and freely and responsibly determines himself in so far as he surpasses himself, projecting and losing himself beyond himself.[37] It is through being the heart and centre of his own transcendence in this way that man constitutes himself a source of values, thus replacing God by himself as the creative ground of intelligibility and meaning: thereby he exercizes his freedom and finds himself again in his freedom.[38] It is not that he chooses freedom; rather is he a freedom which chooses, a freedom that is not free not to be free, just as it is not free not to exist. With a view to saving this freedom Sartre absolutizes contingence to the point where it has to be 'nihilated' in its facticity in order to remain pure. Contingent though he is, there is a sense in which man regarded merely in himself is constrained by the 'factual necessity' of his contingent existence, so that if his freedom is to be sustained it must be through his responsible exertion of 'perpetual contingence' cut off from any reference beyond itself.[39]

Absolute contingence thus replaces in Sartre's view the notion of absolute necessity. It is a contingence empty of all determination other than identity with itself, entirely cut off from any ontological intelligibility of its own and any inter-action with an intelligibility beyond itself. Absolute con-tingence thus collapses in upon itself like a meaningless black hole. This extreme radicalization of contingence is carried out through rethinking the relation of being to non-being which Sartre finds to be perpetually present inside as well as outside of being. 'Nothingness haunts being'.[40] 'It supposes all being in order to rise up in the heart of being as a hole'.[41] The significant point is that Sartre, unlike other philosophers ancient or modern, gives nothing a determinate place and function *within* the realm of being, but further that he finds that place and function not so much in the objective realm of things in themselves as in the subjective realm of the human *consciousness*.[42] It is indeed because nothingness arises in the heart of man that the human reality is forced to make itself, instead of merely being itself, but as such man is the being within the world through whom the threat of nothingness emerges in it, and by implication disorder also. Thus through this utterly contingent existence of man for himself, cut off from God, there is posited in the very heart of immanence 'a transcendent nothing' to replace the transcendent God as the ultimate ground of being and its intelligibility.[43] If this is the role of nothingness in the consciousness of man whose responsibility it is to exert himself to take the place of God in giving order to everything, it is difficult not to conclude that in the last analysis Sartre's absolutizing of contingence falls back into sheer nothingness and meaninglessness.

It is certainly to the merit of Sartre that he has been able to see beyond the identification of contingency merely with singularity, individuality, or particularity, and to identify contingence as a property of the universe as a whole and throughout its parts—although his largely negative approach to being did not allow him to appreciate the relation of contingence through unique and singular events to the perpetual novelty as well as the rich variety manifested in nature. Moreover, while he perceived that contingence belongs to the essential nature of the universe which it possesses as of inalienable right, he had no concept of contingent order of an ontological kind, which was fatal; for, reduced to brute self-identity and bereft of any stabilizing inner intelligibility, contingence is unable to resist the menace of nothingness. Thus the great lesson to be gained from Sartre's atheistic *tour de force* is that the notion of contingence, deprived of any inner ontological intelligibility and of any semantic reference to intelligibility beyond itself, collapses into disorder and pointlessness. By its very nature contingence is intelligible and a basic source of intelligibility only if it is incomplete in itself and only as it exposes its own intelligibility through being completed beyond itself. That is to say, to be meaningful contingence must have only a relative and not an absolute independence, for absolute independence would alienate it from any signitive or semantic function. The contribution of Sartre and similar existentialists to the notion of contingence lies in their insistance that it must be given a fundamental place in our understanding of the nature of worldly reality and in our appreciation of whatever order we can make of it, and that this is impossible unless our grasp of contingency can be emancipated from the habitual craving of our culture for necessitarian modes of thought. The paradoxical fact, however, is that necessitarianism seemed to be so glued to the back of his mind that Sartre could not think of the relation of a transcendent God to the world except in a necessitarian way, and thereby failed to appreciate that there could be a rational bearing of God upon the universe which, instead of menacing it and negating its freedom or undermining its self-identity, is the continual creative source of its contingent intelligibility and of its astonishing freedom and variety. It is to the consideration of this theological understanding of contingence in its relation to God that we must now turn, for it cannot but affect our basic conception of disorder as well as order.

How are we from the perspective of Christian theology to think of this rational bearing of God upon the universe, and how are we to think of the contingence and order of created reality to which it gives rise?

1. The relation of God to the universe, both in creating it and in unceasingly sustaining it, is an utterly free activity of divine grace, which we have to think of as neither necessary nor arbitrary, but as issuing from transcendent grounds of reason and will in God himself. In the nature of the case we know this, in the measure in which it is possible for us, only by divine revelation and not in any demonstrative or *a priori* way of ourselves. And since the self-revelation of God to us has taken the concrete form of Jesus Christ in whom the eternal mind and will and grace of God are incarnate in human form, and thus are made accessible to human knowing, we formulate and test such statements as the above about the relation of God to the universe by reference to a centre in Christ, in the conviction that what God is toward us in Jesus Christ he is consistently in himself in all his bearing upon the universe he has made. In freely giving himself as the object of our knowledge in Jesus Christ God enables us to know him freely in such a way that he does not have to be known by us when he is known and therefore in such a way that we may fail in knowing him; but when we do know him in response to his self-revelation we find that our knowledge of him is controlled beyond itself in the rationality of God. That is to say, God does not import any necessity or arbitrariness into his relations with us, and yet he remains throughout contingently related to us in his grace so that our relation to him correspondingly takes the form of freedom and faith. That is the Christological ground of our belief that God's relation to the universe from beginning to end is neither necessary nor arbitrary but one of ceaseless freedom and grace issuing out of his eternal mind and will of love. By its very nature, this gratuitous contingent activity of God in creating and sustaining the universe is incomprehensible to us, for we are unable to compare it with, or construe it in terms of, anything we may claim already to know, but we have to reckon with it as the initially given. Here we have to do with a belief in God's rational bearing upon the universe which, to borrow words from Norman Kemp Smith, we must regard not as 'a minimum belief' but as 'a maximum belief', which 'commits us to all the many other beliefs congruent with, and consequent upon, itself'.[44] Thus, as John Duns Scotus pointed out many

centuries ago, belief in the contingent relation betv
and the world commits us to the conviction that all
tenets of the Christian faith have to do, not with n
but with contingent acts of God, which we express ... such
contingent statements as 'God created the world', 'the Son
of God became man', or 'Jesus Christ died and rose again'.[45]
This basic belief, however, also obliges us to hold that the
contingence of the world is itself grounded in the utterly
contingent activity of God's grace in freely giving being to,
and sustaining in being, all reality other than God himself.
Hence if the contingence of the universe regarded in its own
givenness is found to be mysterious and baffling, that must
surely be traced back to the inexplicable grace and contingence of God's creativity.

2. Brought into being by the contingent activity of God in
this way, the creation must be regarded as a manifestation
of divine grace—not that it is itself that grace but the result
of it which bears the imprint of divine grace in its contingent
character. Thus the rational bearing of the Creator upon the
universe, far from imposing any prior or final necessity upon
it or denying to it any freedom of its own, grounds it upon
his own transcendent freedom in such a way as to endow it
with a contingent freedom, functioning *sua natura*, as the
Reformation theologians used to say, and creatively correlates
it with his own uncreated rationality in such a way that it is
endowed with an indeterminate range of possibility in its
own natural processes. It is precisely in virtue of the contingent freedom thus given to it that the creation constantly
manifests a capacity for change and development through
novel variations that surprise and astonish us. As such the
universe is to be regarded as a created reflection of the
unlimited freedom of the Creator.

3. The contingency of the creation as it derives from God is
inseparably bound up with its orderliness, for it is the product
not merely of his almighty will but of his eternal reason. It
is not only the matter of the universe, therefore, but its form
that comes into being out of nothing, for under the rational
creativity of God matter and form are fused indivisibly
together from the very beginning. There is no contingence
without order and no order without contingence, for contingence is inherently orderly and order is essentially contingent.

This means that the contingence of the universe is not to be understood in the final analysis as sheer facticity without any inner determination or as brute fact with some kind of order extrinsically impressed upon it, as if in our scientific understanding of them facts were only laden with theory and were not already constituted in themselves, independent of our knowing of them, through an ontological integration of empirical and theoretical factors. Moreover, under the ceaseless creative bearing of God upon the universe, this integration is to be understood not as a static or predetermined programming but as a dynamic functioning of its contingent processes in a mutual involution of form and being, giving rise to ever richer patterns of order which may be understood only in terms of their natural onto-relational structures.

4. The creative bearing of God upon the universe, through which he provides in his own divine freedom and rationality the stable ground of the freedom and rationality of created reality, gives contingence a double aspect. Contingence has at once an orientation toward God in dependence on him, and an orientation away from God in a relative independence of him. Both aspects belong to God's creative purpose for the universe which he approves as good and which he continuously confirms in the unbroken ontological relation that he maintains between the creation and himself. Orientation toward God may be regarded as the positive aspect of contingence, for it is from God that the universe derives its being and order, while orientation away from God may be regarded as the negative aspect of contingence, for it implies that if the universe were left entirely to itself it would be without being or order. But if they are so regarded they cannot be taken as logical or dialectical contraries, for far from being exclusive of one another they imply one another. The very dependence of the universe upon the transcendent freedom and rationality of God gives it a contingent freedom and rationality of its own, whereas the freedom and rationality which the creation has in its own natural right or independence are significant in their contingent nature only as they are incomplete and have reference beyond themselves—apart from that reference they would lose their contingence and could only decompose and disappear within a circle of

necessitarian and meaningless self-reference. It is thus essential to the integrity and significance of contingence that both aspects, contingence on God and contingence from God, dependence on God and independence of him, condition one another in a counterpoised relation between them.

It is important to note, however, that what we have called the negative aspect of contingence in no sense negates the positive aspect but fulfils its function within the positive, thereby contributing itself positively to the full nature of contingence. In its orientation away from God, the one self-sufficient being and the creative source of all other being, the contingent universe borders on non-being and chaos, so that from that direction there would appear to be a natural threat to the being of the universe if it were left to itself. Contingent reality has thus an intrinsic fragility and lability: without stability of its own, it is evanescent. That is to say, if God were to terminate his creative upholding of the universe, if he were to withdraw from it his immanent presence whereby he undergirds and supports the being of the universe in order to realize its positive relation to himself, the universe would collapse and disintegrate into nothing. But since God has made the universe contingent, and does not negate it but positively affirms it in its contingent state, the bordering of the universe on non-being and chaos does not as such menace the universe or threaten it with destruction, but is an essential constituent of its good autonomy as contingent reality. It is precisely in this contingent fragility and lability that the universe has been established by God and is maintained by him in his unremitting faithfulness, so that the very fact that the universe constantly hovers on the verge of non-being or that it is evidently corruptible and always in peril of passing away, is not to be marked down as an imperfection but rather as belonging to the perfection of contingent existence. This is another way of saying that the created universe exists by the grace of God: far from being a weakness, that is its strength and glory in God.

Since the relation of the world to God, wherein he constitutes himself as its ultimate ground and sufficient reason, rests on the free contingent activity of his grace, and is not necessary, it can neither be taken for granted nor be compellingly demonstrated by us. Hence, as Karl Barth has pointed out, the relation of the world to God cannot be understood or derived from empty general concepts of God but only from the actualization of God's grace in positive interaction with us, as in the incarnation, passion, and resurrection of Jesus Christ his eternal Word through whom all things were made, whereby he illumines the creation for us and allows us to understand something of its distinctive nature from the perspective of his creative and ordering relation to it in grace.[46] Contemplated apart from such specific acts of divine revelation and communication, however, the creation presents to us a highly ambiguous appearance precisely because of the double face of contingence, toward God and away from God. This is why, evidently, the usual arguments from contingence and design are so ambivalent, equally poised one way or the other, for relation to God or for absence of relation to God. Certainly if we logicalize the arguments and thus operate with necessary relations of thought we may do away with ambiguity, but we would eliminate contingent relations and so lose any semantic reference of the world to its Creator. In any case there can be no logical bridge between the universe and God, any more than there can be a logical bridge between the theoretic concepts of natural science and the ontic structures of the empirical world disclosed to science through its inquiries.

If the semantic reference of the universe is not to remain ambiguous for us in that it points both toward God and away from him, the contingent order of the universe would need to be intersected by the arc of a higher-level order in God himself, in such a way that its incomplete signification is completed by positive content in God. Far from undermining our understanding of the natural order of the universe, which is contingently correlated to God by the grace of creation, this intersection would have the effect of recognizing and affirming it in its distinctively contingent status, while bringing it into a contrapuntal relation, so to speak, to the divine order which has moved directly into our world in Jesus Christ the incarnate Word of God and constitutes the *canto firmo* whereby the fleeting and fragile contingent signification is integrated and elevated to terminate at its proper end in God himself. This would seem to imply that in so far as the secrets of the contingent order of the universe functioning *sua natura* may yield to natural scientific inquiry, they may be correlated helpfully with an understanding of that contingent order functioning *dei gratia* mediated through theological inquiry. However it may also imply that without the insight derived from such a correlation, the interpretation by natural science of the distinctively contingent nature of the order of the universe may stumble on its ambiguity, so that it is tempted to iron it out into determinate formalizations of regularities and continuities in nature, thereby rationalizing away its contingent reference beyond the universe itself.

iii. Disorder

Now that we have considered so fully the nature of contingence and the place given to it in our theological and scientific thought, we must take up the question of 'disorder' or 'evil' which has already arisen at several significant points in the foregoing discussion, and give it direct attention. Does the contingent universe disclose to our investigations only orderly patterns in nature, or do we find irrational elements in it disrupting order?

It is important to see right away that any question about disorder or evil, physical or moral, is caught in an inherent difficulty. The very notion of disorder or evil entails the idea of a breach in regularity or a break in continuity, which we cannot even entertain in thought without reference to regularity or continuity. To think rationally and scientifically we have to think in terms of regularities and continuities, but when we are asked to think of what is irregular or discontinuous our rational and scientific determinations of mind make us think it away, for the coherent continuity of our thought carries it across the discontinuities. If the disorder or evil is only superficial we will doubtless find a way of scrambling it out as some sort of irrelevant incidental 'noise'; but if it is radical, a gaping chasm in being and order which we cannot rationally span, is not the rational thing to do to suspend our habit of thinking only in regularities or continuities, much as we would rein to a halt a galloping horse before an ugly big ditch which it could not jump? How does one think a chasm or a hole in the continuity of being? Is that the impasse which some of our radical existentialists have reached, when they insist on trying to think 'nothing' or on taking a blind leap into 'nothing'?—which would seem to be no more than an empty and irrational movement of thought! The existentialist answer to the problem is meant to be serious, but it rests, as we have seen, upon the unacceptable assumption that there is no objective order beyond or within the universe and no order at all other than what we are able to make of things. Nor will it do to think of the impasse as posed by Schelling, who argued that if we are to retain a unitary (or, as in his case, a monist) view of the universe we must regard evil as ontologically somewhat superficial, but if we regard evil as radical we must give up any hope of being able to offer a logically coherent account of the universe.[47] The problem is deeper than that, however, for whether evil is superficial or radical, no rational, and certainly no logical, explanation of it can be given, for we cannot think discontinuity by continuity without rationalizing or logicalizing it away. The actual situation is this: evil would present no problem to us at all—we would not even be aware of it—if there were no objective and coherent rational order, for what 'constitutes' evil 'evil' is its contradiction of objective order on the one hand and its negation by that objective order on the other hand. Evil rises up and confronts us, disturbing and entangling us in its strange impossible actuality. How are we to understand it, or rather, how are we really to understand the understanding we already have of it?

It is the claim of Christian theology that some measure of understanding evil is possible, because the objective divine order of the good and rational does not merely negate evil but lays hold of it in a re-creative and re-ordering movement with a view to mastering it, repairing what is disordered, and making it serve a fuller dimension of order than might have been possible otherwise. This is not to claim that evil may be explained in any way—quite the contrary—but that God himself has acted in the incarnation, passion and resurrection of his Son Jesus Christ, in such a way as to deal decisively with the actuality of evil where it has entrenched itself in the depths of created existence and to overcome its alienating and disruptive movement, shoring up from below, as it were, the divisions and discontinuities which have erupted into the world. It is because the ontological and epistemological situation has been altered in that way, that Christian theology ventures to say something definite about evil which could not be said from any other ground. But it does so only with a prayer for forgiveness for blindness and error, in the realization that the presence of evil continues to damage our relations with God, with the world, and with one another, so that our thought is characterized by a certain brokenness which does not allow us to think the truth through consistently to its proper end.[48] It is especially when the subject of evil enters into the reference that theological concepts suffer from that kind of refraction, which is why eschatological factors inevitably condition what we may think or say about redemption from evil or the final triumph of God over it.

It is above all in the Cross of Christ that evil is unmasked for what it actually is, in its inconceivable wickedness and malevolence, in its sheer contradiction of the love of God incarnate in Jesus Christ, in its undiluted enmity to God himself—not to mention the way in which it operates under the cover of the right and the good and the lawful. That the infinite God should take the way of the Cross to save mankind from the pit of evil which has engulfed it and deceived it, is the measure of the evil of evil: its depth is revealed to be 'abysmal' (literally, 'without bottom'). However, it is only from the vantage point of God's victory over evil in the resurrection of Christ, from the bridge which in him God has thrown across the chasm of evil that has opened up in our violence and death and guilt, that we may look into the full horror of it all and not be destroyed in the withering of our souls through misanthropy, pessimism, and despair. What hope could there ever be for a humanity that crucifies the incarnate love of God and sets itself implacably against the order of divine love even at the point of its atoning and healing operation? But the resurrection tells us that evil, even this abysmal evil, does not and cannot have the last word, for that belongs to the love of God which has negated evil once and for all and which through the Cross and resurrection is able to make all things work together for good, so that nothing in the end will ever separate us from the love of God. It is from the heart of that love in the resurrected Son of God that we may reflect on the radical nature of evil without suffering morbid mesmerization or pathological distortion. But the sheer physicality of the resurrection and crucifixion events, which belong inseparably together, has behind it the incarnation, the staggering fact that God himself has come directly into our creaturely being to become one of us, for our sakes. Thus the incarnation, passion, and resurrection conjointly tell us that far from evil having to do only with human hearts and minds, it has become entrenched in the ontological depths of created existence and that it is only from within those ontological depths that God could get at the heart of evil in order to destroy it, and set about rebuilding what he had made to be good. (We have to think of that as the only way that God 'could' take, for the fact that he has as a matter of fact taken this way in the freedom of his grace excludes any other possibility from our consideration.) It is surely in the light of this ontological salvation that we are to understand the so-called 'nature miracles', as well as the resurrection of Jesus from death, for they represent not a suspension of the natural or created order but the very reverse, the recreation of the natural order wherever it suffers from decay or damage or corruption or disorder through evil. God does not give up his claim that the creation is 'good', but insists on upholding that claim by incarnating within the creation the personal presence of his own Logos, the creative and ordering source of the creation, thereby pledging his own eternal constancy and rationality as the ground for the redemption and final establishment of all created reality.

This theological approach to the question of evil understandably moves from the context of moral evil in human existence, but, as we can see, it has implications which reach beyond that context into the physical universe of which man himself is an essential constituent. Since it is through man's interaction with the physical universe that its empirical and contingent order comes to rational expression, it is not unlikely that, man being the kind of being he is, any physical evil or disorder that may emerge will also have to do with his interaction with the physical universe. However, is evil evil only in man's experience of it, or is it something also that he experiences as independent of himself but which he intensifies in his interaction with it? Clearly no sharp line between moral or human evil and physical evil can be drawn. Certainly the Christian concepts of the salvation of the whole man and of the renewal of the whole creation imply that there are elements of physical evil or disorder in the universe. If this is the case, how is it to be related to our discussion of contingent order?

As we have already had occasion to note, a theology operating from a central point of reference in Christ—the incarnate Word of God by whom all things were made and in whom all things consist—could not hold contingence to be a defect or imperfection in the universe but rather to be a distinctive property of its creaturely perfection. Hence there must be ruled out any idea that evil belongs to contingent being as such, for that would be tantamount to denying that what God has made he has made to be good, as well as charging him with defective handiwork. There must also be ruled out the idea that evil is bound up with the negative aspect of contingence and inevitably arises out of it, for that would split apart the negative and positive aspects of contingence, making nonsense of it as well as implying that contingent reality is not inherently orderly. There is some limited justification for the Augustinian-Thomist view that evil is a privation of the good and a defection from being, for evil can have no independent existence of its own, but is that view, in part at least, not a way of trying to explain evil by drawing a line of continuity below or through any discontinuity that may appear, thus in the last resort rationalizing discontinuity away? Behind the Augustinian-Thomist approach, however, lies an inadequate notion of contingence, together with an absence of any real notion of contingent order; but there also lies behind it an inadequate appreciation of the gravity of evil. Face to face with the crucifixion of the Son of God, it does not seem at all possible to agree that the evil manifested there was no more than an absence of the good. Whatever the full implications of the New Testament statements about 'demonic forces', 'powers of darkness', 'Satan', or 'the fearful enmity of the carnal heart of man towards God', it is undoubtedly

implied that in the passion of Christ there took place a
terribly real and anguished struggle on the part of God
incarnate with something utterly sinister and relentlessly
hostile, from which emerged the realization by Christian
thought that evil is an assault upon the love of God, an
attack upon the majesty and prerogative of the Creator, an
anarchic force making for the vitiation and destruction of all
that is true and good and orderly in God's creation. There is
no suggestion in the evangelical message that evil might be
explained, even in part, either by reference to the Creator or
by reference to the creature as its author. That is why evil is
linked to the forces of darkness upon which God has, as it
were, turned his back, not the 'darkness' that results from the
infinite excess of divine light over creaturely light throwing it
comparatively 'into the dark', but the darkness of a malevolent falsehood and irrationality. Evil remains an utterly
inexplicable 'mystery' (as the Bible speaks of it), but a
fearful actuality, nevertheless, which must be totally and
consistently opposed by man as it is by God.[49]

May evil be regarded, then, as something like 'anti-being'
that has unexplainably irrupted into created existence, that
is, as a direct negation of being rather than as a mere defection
from being? Certainly evil is found breaking into creaturely
being, introducing disorder and bringing about ontological
collapse, yet the creature becomes so identified with this
evil that it willingly revolts from the Creator in a suicidal
movement to break off its independence from dependence
on him, and thereby lurches toward non-being. It is the
intertwining of evil with the act and being of the creature
that is so difficult to grasp and express, for while evil does
not originate from creaturely being as such, but enters in as
an alien invader, it nevertheless becomes rooted in the
creature in such a way that the creature becomes evil and
does evil of itself. To revert to a use of personal terms, it is
not merely that the human being sins against God and his
neighbour, but that he becomes and *is* a sinner so that his
sinful acts arise out of his own heart and mind. Yet this evil
which the creature makes his own could have no natural
counterpoise within his being, such as the negative aspect
has in the positive aspect of contingent being, for it is alien
and unnatural. Evil should be regarded, however, as latching

on to the negative aspect in contingent existence or its natural independence, thus getting a hold within it and functioning in such a way as to alienate the negative from the positive aspect of contingence; that is, contingence from God is wrenched away from contingence toward God. In bringing about this break between the creature and the Creator evil disrupts the inner equilibrium of contingent order and causes the collapse of contingent existence toward nothingness.

Of course if the alienation of contingent reality from God were wholly actualized, if the universe were to achieve autonomy from its Creator, it would disappear entirely into nothing. However, in so far as that alienation is held in suspense or blocked by the divine opposition to evil, so that in spite of evil the ontological relation between the creation and the Creator is preserved, then we must think of the universe as upheld in a sort of half-alienation, or fixed in its damaged condition and locked in its autonomy—i.e. the state of creation which theologians speak of as 'the Fall'. In that event the universe could not but become opaque, for the semantic reference of its contingent order would be refracted and bent, and the Creator would be obscured from his creation—hence the 'brokenness' which we find in the lines we attempt to project from the natural order of things toward the Creator.

This way of thinking of evil would appear to be truer to what evil is actually found to be in our experience, a direct negation of being and goodness rather than a defection from being and a privation of goodness, but it is not without its danger for it runs the risk of a kind of dualism.[50] Yet this 'anti-being', as we have called it, can have no independent ground of existence over against God who is the sole source of being, and who precisely as God rejects evil with all his Godness—for by being God he excludes all that is anti-God. When we ask, therefore, what kind of existence does evil or this anti-being have, we can only say that it 'is' what God negates—an 'improper existence', which Karl Barth has called an 'impossible possibility'. Whatever sort of actuality evil may have—and it is certainly very actual—it can have only a desperate quasi-existence or perverse reality under the ban of the divine rejection which leaves evil with no substance or perpetuity of its own. The actualization of that rejection in our space–time existence has taken place once and for all in the death and resurrection of Jesus Christ, through which evil has been judged, denied the power to 'nihilate' the creation and its order, and is destined for complete overthrow. Meantime, while all creation is in an agony of suspense and expectation waiting for that final end, evil is paradoxically and marvellously made to serve the purpose of God's love for his creatures.

From the perspective of Christian theology, then, it would appear that evil and the menace of nothingness cannot be regarded as confined to the human and moral sphere, for in Jesus Christ God has shown that his saving and recreating work comprehends all creation. From the perspective of natural science, however, we must ask whether there is any evidence for physical evil in nature or in the universe. What about decay, decomposition, and death, and what about entropy? This is not altogether a straight-forward question, for if we did not believe that God is good and that the temporal order of things he has conferred upon the universe serves his good will, we would have no problem with decay, decomposition, and death, or with entropy, nor would we find affliction and suffering intolerable for they would be treated merely as part of the natural process of things. Yet, as we have seen, even though natural science must pursue its inquiries into the structures and patterns latent in the universe in an attempt to grasp its intrinsic order and ration-ality, without reference to God or the contingence of the universe upon God, it cannot grapple with questions of contingent order if they are cut off entirely from dependence on God. Even though it must assume contingence as an operational factor to be reckoned with in all experimental questioning of nature, it is ultimately faced with the ground of its intelligibility beyond the finite conditions of nature especially as the inquiries of natural science are pressed to the very edge of contingent realities where they border on nothing. It is because natural science operates with an un-defined assumption behind all its acceptance of an orderly universe, which bears on God and his goodness, that the scientist is also troubled about questions of evil and the disruption of order. Hence he cannot be entirely satisfied with the claim that decay, decomposition, and death are merely aspects of contingence, that is, in this context, that they relate to the property which physical entities have of passing away, or of irreversible temporality. This involves what used to be called the principle of the degradation of energy or what we now think of as the principle of increasing entropy as defined by the second law of thermodynamics.

It must be noted, however, that entropy cannot be merely equated with disorder. Although decay, decomposition, and death represent the dissolution of certain states of order and a descent into a condition of static equilibrium or uniformity or immobility, nevertheless if the universe were not characterized by a unidirectional increase in entropy, if time were reversible, no steady change or advance in orderly patterns in the universe would be possible. Thus the equation of entropy and disorder needs to be counterbalanced by the recognition that the principle of increasing entropy, as classically formulated, holds only within a closed system and cannot apply to the universe as a whole or to its constant development in the emergence of richer and more complex forms of order, and by the recognition that for change and increase in order to take place there must always be latent in the orderly patterns of nature a measure of entropy resisting necessitation or fixation in order. There must be a degree of non-closure, incompleteness or openness allowing for new possibilities in which event statistical probability would replace mechanical computation. That is to say, thermodynamically regarded, 'order' and 'disorder' condition one another and together make for the orderly advance or development which we find in nature. Instead of equating entropy with disorder, therefore, it should be represented as the logarithm of probability. It is evidently in this direction that there is now taking place, notably through the work of Ilya Prigogine, a significant reconstruction and application of thermodynamic theory to open or non-equilibrium systems, in which it is shown that fluctuations arising far from a state of equilibrium are not finally elements of chaos or disorder but rather factors actually giving rise to new and richer forms of order.[51] This is an extension of scientific thought which enables us, in some measure at least, to account for the upward gradient of orderly development in the universe against the downward process of increasing entropy.[52]

In this event it is understandable that natural science should regard decay, decomposition, and death as having more to do with thermodynamic change through the balance in the exchange of matter and energy between entities and their environment within the limits of the finite universe, than with anything that may be held to be evil. They are natural features and functions of contingent existence which do not admit of the idealizing operations of mathematico-scientific method, and which exhibit natural limits within which natural science may not transgress without importing distortion. It is, therefore, the combining of thermodynamic and relativity theory which, by halting or restricting idealization, preserves in our understanding the natural properties of contingence and contingent order.

Let that be granted, but the question must still be raised whether evil elements have infiltrated these functions and features of nature, thereby giving them a malignant twist which makes them 'disorderly' in an irrational way. Of course so long as idealization holds sway any elements of irrational disorder or evil in nature could hardly be 'evident' to natural science which would inevitably juggle them out of the way, as it were, under the axiomatic drive for symmetries and equilibria. The situation is somewhat changed with the injection of relativity into thermodynamic theory and the discovery of transformation equations enabling thought to move from equilibrium systems to non-equilibrium systems in which we have to do with dynamic states of matter and their open-structured organizations which defy complete formalization and which, in so far as they may be formalized, require incomplete symbols. However, prompted by our ultimate belief that the universe is everywhere pervaded by rational order—which we cannot allow to be questioned without committing our reason to a sort of suicide—we tend instinctively to overlook or explain away any awkward or surd-like elements in nature upon which our inquiries may stumble. Nevertheless, there are problems which we cannot easily shrug off, not least the predator-prey syndrome at the heart of the evolutionary process, and indeed sheer animal pain. Are these only ingredients in the functioning of animal survival-mechanisms and of orderly development, or do they contain elements which we cannot but regard as evil? What of the fact that creatures exist by devouring one another, and of the endless waste of life in the universe at all levels of sentient and organic life? What of needless arbitrary suffering like cruelty which shocks our sense of rightness and goodness? It is difficult not to think that somehow nature has been infiltrated by an extrinsic evil, affecting entropy for ill, corrupting natural processes, and introducing irrational kinks into their order, so that it is hardly surprising that even the ablest scientists can be overwhelmed by the pointlessness of it all.[53]

If evil has somehow overtaken the processes of nature, we would have to think of it as intruding a disturbing breach into the balance of contingent existence, setting the negative aspect of contingence at variance with its positive aspect. This means that the apparent threat of the negative aspect to contingent existence, if left to itself, would be turned into an actual menace, obstructive of its order and destructive of its being. Decay, decomposition, and death could not then be regarded as merely natural features and functions but as charged with anti-natural elements, perverting natural corruptibility into a degenerate force and giving natural entropy a dysteleological twist at odds with the expansion of nature toward higher and more complex forms of organization.

To a large extent this state of affairs in animal existence must remain problematic for us since we are unable to understand what evil may mean merely at the animal level. However, some light may be shed on it from our own human participation in decay, decomposition, and death as they have been affected by 'the Fall', i.e., by man's estrangement from God resulting from his sin in seeking to make himself independent of him. Here there has opened up in man's existence a gulf of corruption and perdition which threatens to swallow him up, but that does not altogether happen. God refuses to be estranged from man or to forego his claim over him, and so he does not allow man to fall completely away from him, but continues to sustain him in being even in his fallen condition as the creature which he had made to be 'good'. Thus by continuing to love man and by insisting on reclaiming him, God opposes man's self-will and self-isolation, rejects the evil that has overtaken him and negates the corruption lodged in his existence, which has the effect of bringing the divine judgement to bear upon man not only in his inward being but wherever the rupture in his relations with God is actualized in his physical existence—in decay, decomposition, and death.

Several aspects of this human predicament call for comment. Evil is now so interwoven with what man is in will and act, in his spiritual and physical existence, that sin and corruption are ultimately inseparable. Hence it is with the whole man that God interacts in his rejection of evil, so that man lives and dies under the threat of destruction, not only from the negation of evil, but from the negation of the divine judgement upon it. Human corruption and death, therefore, are to be treated not merely as the natural outcome of man's contingent fragile existence but also as the inexorable outworking of the divine opposition to the evil that has invaded and taken hold of human being—that is what evidently lies at the root of man's anxiety and dread. However, behind this 'No' of God's judgement upon man there is the mighty unalterable 'Yes' of God's unconditional love for man which negates his corruption and death, repudiates all estrangement between the creature and the Creator, and ontologically embraces man in the grace and life of God himself. Thus, far from allowing evil to drag man down through decay, decomposition, and death into sheer disintegration and annihilation, God overrules all that evil can inflict on human existence, making it to serve his supreme purpose of creation and redemption. He triumphs, retrospectively and prospectively, over the futility and pointlessness to which man appears to be subjected by evil, redirecting human existence through all suffering and pain to a far more blessed and incorruptible end.

In view of this human experience it would be difficult not to believe that God is also opposed to evil in animal existence and all the suffering and pain it brings in its train, and that God in his universal purpose of creation and redemption will not allow his non-human creation to be wasted. While evil may be at work dissolving the creature's relation to God, it cannot dissolve the will of God to uphold what he has made in the face of all that threatens to disintegrate it, and therefore evil cannot succeed in subtracting the creature from the ontological support of the Creator or from his purpose for it. We must surely believe that God does not let his creation break free from his control only to plunge down some slope of degeneration or disorder too steep for it to be reclaimed, but that in his divine wisdom and creative power he directs it from a higher level of order in such a way that he makes any obstruction or evil misdirection immanent in nature to serve a fuller and richer end than might have been otherwise possible.

This account of things in nature clearly presupposes the doctrine of creation, that the universe received its manifold order as well as its existence from beyond it altogether, from God the Creator. It is on the ground of the same assumption that we may hold that the universe as a whole retains its orderly arrangements through interaction with a creative source of order beyond it. If we think of the universe only in itself—in its contingence away from God—with no system or environment beyond it with which it could exchange matter and energy in order to keep going, then we would have to think of it as inexorably running down through steadily increasing entropy toward a state of complete equilibrium and final 'death', in accordance with the requirements of the second law of thermodynamics as classically formulated. However, this seems to present us with the greatest of difficulties, for then we would have to hold that the orderly states and morphological arrangements, above all in living organisms, found in the universe, came entirely from unlimited chance or random fluctuations, but, so far as we can compute the time required for all this to have come about (1, millions of zeros!), the universe would have to be many, many times older than we know it to be. That is to say, time-dependent laws of probability exclude this kind of explanation by chance developments completely. *A fortiori* this would apply to the emergence of the higher animals only some four or five hundred million years after the appearance of the most primitive invertebrates! Doubtless here in natural science we reach a turning point, for evidently we have no way within the universe of accounting for the increase in the order of its systems so long as the laws of thermodynamics are restricted in their application only to closed or equilibrium systems requiring an increase in entropy to compensate for any temporal increase in order. Even when these laws are applied to open or non-equilibrium systems we have to think of the emergence of order as taking place 'spontaneously', for the explanations that can be offered are partial and have only a limited validity. When we consider the universe as a whole, however, we seem to reach a clear impasse—in some respects not unlike the so-called 'event horizon' that halts our thought at the perimeter of a 'black hole' where our laws cease to apply. Thus, while the laws of thermodynamics state that physical systems are finally over-taken by disorder owing to the inevitable increase in entropy, the range of their validity is shown to be limited by the fact that there has been throughout the history of the expanding universe, and still is, a constant advance in overall order. Hence we have no way, either, of accounting for the increase in the order of the universe regarded as a whole, yet this order must derive from somewhere, presumably from 'outside' the universe. It will not do to claim that this order is to be traced back solely to the original programming of the universe in its initial conditions, for, true as that might be, we would still have to ask where all that stored-up order came from.[54] If on the other hand, we claim that it came from 'outside' the universe—which would seem the only alternative left to us—the universe must be redefined as incomplete, i.e. not as embracing all that is, beyond which by definition there is nothing at all, but as embracing only all that is contingent and finite; and this in turn would require contingence and finitude to be included as essential factors in our formulation of all thermodynamic law. Rather than think of the universe as completely self-contained, therefore, let theology introduce into the cosmic equation an extra and extrinsic term, the creative interaction of God with the universe which he has made. Then we may be in a position to offer some rational account, not only for the original conditions making for order in the expanding uni-verse, but for the stability and constancy of order and its development against the persistent downward drag of entropy.[55]

Be that as it may for the universe as a whole, within the universe itself we must surely operate with the principle of directive control between the many levels of order which, as we have seen, characterize the stratified structure of the universe. Each level remains 'indeterminate' or 'uncertain' or 'incomplete' in such a way that it is open at its boundary conditions to external direction from another level. Thus the kind of order that obtains at each level is found not to be of a necessary but of a contingent kind which cannot be understood from a framework of rigid determinism without being distorted. In any pair of levels of order interaction between them contributes an essential ingredient to the nature of the order on each level. This may be looked at in two ways, depending on the vantage point provided by one or other level, for example, in the interaction between a physical and a biotic level. If we look at it from the 'lower' level of physico-chemical relations we find that the full potential of their organization is activated only through interaction with the 'higher' level of biological relations. Thus instead of being confined to itself, the physico-chemical level of order contributes the ground conditions for a more complex form of order, that of living organisms beyond it, and really becomes meaningful in the rational structure of nature when it fulfils that rôle. If we look at it from the 'higher' level of biological relations, on the other hand, we find that through its interaction with, and control over the boundary conditions of, the 'lower' level, an organismic order is imposed on it, as the contribution of the 'lower' level to the 'higher' is made to serve a pattern and function, and indeed a 'purpose', of which it is incapable in itself. Thus at one and the same time the interaction of the 'higher' level with the 'lower' limits the range of its validity and enlarges its scope for development. This is what happens, for example, when a quantity of inert matter is artificially made to embody an aeronautical design which allows it to be harnessed and controlled by a set of engineering principles beyond its physico-chemical level, so that it can take flight as an aeroplane. The laws of physics and chemistry are not infringed but they are restricted and made to serve an end beyond what they can account for in terms of themselves alone. Hence we may hold as a general principle that within the coherent structure of the universe the 'lower' levels of reality disclose the full measure of their proper order when the 'higher' levels interact creatively with them, and conversely that through the interaction of the 'higher' levels with the 'lower' the latter are given direction and purpose within the meaningful organization of the multi-levelled complex of the universe.

iv. Man's Priestly and Redemptive Rôle in the World

We must now return to the question of physical evil or disorder in the universe. At an earlier point we noted that we would have to think of the presence of evil in nature as a disturbing breach intruded into the balance of contingent existence, creating tension between its positive and negative aspects. In view of our present discussion of the stratified coordination of orderly relations in the universe, it would seem reasonable to think of evil in relation to obstruction or failure in the interaction between 'lower' and 'higher' levels of physical reality. This is far from easy, however, even though we may have no difficulty in identifying the effects of evil in nature, as in animal suffering and cruelty. The cross-level two-way interaction in nature gives rise to a dynamic non-linear type of order which is well-nigh impossible to bring to formal expression, even with the help (where it is appropriate) of algebraic matrices or of group theory. Very often, it is thought, the best that one can do is to employ a statistical method of description in the hope of bringing to light invariant patterns exhibited by large groups or aggregates of events. In the nature of the case any interference or obstruction is taken up into the complex of data and tends to be lost in the computation of the average pattern or the law of the group. In so far as these statistical results relate to what happens in nature, and not just to our observations of nature, they would appear to imply that nature has some sort of built-in self-corrective device through which the interaction of the 'higher' levels with the 'lower' redeems them, not only from any meaninglessness or pointlessness they would have if left to themselves, but from any disturbance or disorder that may happen to arise. If so, this would not justify physical evil, but it would indicate that there appears to be operating immanently in nature something corresponding to the divine overruling which we considered as the interaction of God's own power of order with the world he has made, in the course of which the disorder that threatens to overwhelm the creation with meaninglessness and destruction is not only negated but suborned by the love of God and made to serve the fulfilment of a higher and richer order.

From the perspective of theology man is clearly made the focal point in the interrelations between God and the universe. He is given a special place within the creation with a ruling and a priestly function to perform toward the rest of created reality. All lines of rationality and order, of purpose and fulfilment in the creation converge on him as man of God and man of science and depend on his destiny. From the perspective of natural science man must also be recognized to be a focal point of significance in the universe, both because he represents the culmination of its development to ever higher levels of reality and order and because all we know of the universe, even of the universe and its structures billions of years before ever man emerged, is correlated to the rationality of man. There is a profound harmony between the rationality of the human understanding and the rationality of the universe, and indeed a congruence between the stratified structure of science and the stratified structure of nature. If man occupies this place of focal significance in respect of the order of the universe, he must also occupy a place of focal significance in respect of any disorder that arises within it. Hence it will be important for us to consider the problem of evil and disorder in nature by reference to the interaction of man with the rest of creation.

If in any pair of levels of order it is through the interaction of the 'higher' with the 'lower' level that the latter is brought to unfold and develop its inchoate order, and the 'higher' level itself, while relying on the 'lower' and interacting with a still 'higher' level, produces a richer form of rational order, then man's place in the universe has a particular importance for the whole multi-levelled structure. He is, in theological language, 'the crown of creation'. It is as he interacts with God the Creator, thereby really becoming the man he is meant to be, that he can best interact with the various strata of orderly existence 'below' his own and affect their interaction with one another in such a way as to bring out their full potential and enhance their development. Just as nature has been created in such a way that at every level and in every species it produces its own kind, so the universe as a whole is formed in such a way that man constitutes that intelligent ingredient in it through whose heuristic inquiry and creative activity the universe knows and unfolds itself in developing rational order and expression. This is man's priestly function in the universe, as man of faith and man of science. Without him the various levels of contingent reality in the universe would lapse back into meaninglessness and pointlessness, but with and through him the meaning and the purpose of the universe are disclosed and effectuated.

In the event of evil irrupting into the creation introducing disorder into it, this priestly role of man must take on a redemptive form—that is how we should now view man's relation to nature. It is his task to save the natural order through remedial and integrative activity, bringing back order where there is disorder and restoring peace where there is disharmony. Since it is through interaction with man, the culminating point of rational order, that nature unfolds and develops its possibilities, it should not only be 'pacified' through man, for example, in being saved from disease and suffering, not least in the levels of animal existence, but in a significant sense be 'humanized'—that is, through human cultivation and development nature should bring forth forms of order and beauty of which it would not be capable otherwise. However, when man himself is seized of evil, and his interaction with the Creator is damaged and disordered, his interaction with nature becomes damaged and disordered as well. Something very different takes place, for the whole balance of nature is upset. That is the sad story of ecological chaos with which we are only too familiar, a disorderly state of affairs in nature brought about by man's disrespectful and greedy exploitation of the natural order for his own, now rather twisted, ends. This is not to say that nature is not also greatly enhanced by man or that new levels of order have not already been realized through human cultivation and development, but that man continually infects nature with his own disorder even in the midst of these priestly and redemptive operations. It would also be true to say that in and through the profound interconnection of order and disorder in which man and nature share together, nature constantly reveals surprising new possibilities in spite of man, which can have a healing and rectifying effect on him, for after all it is much more in man himself than in nature that evil has lodged itself.

It must be acknowledged that in the modern world the so-called 'technological society' is often found betraying the integrity of science by deploying its undoubted power for ideological or imperialistic ends, and therein is also found to be sinning against the integrity of the creation. This has largely to do with the interference of man in the harmonies of the empirical order and the subjection of nature to violent devices, with unforeseen consequences often of a dire kind, such as disturbance and imbalance in our physical environment. On the one hand, it cuts off man from nature, damaging his proper interaction with the other levels of physical reality and their rectifying integrations. And as a result man himself is often trapped in the instruments of manipulation he has created—as we can see again and again in the Marxist substitution of technology for science. On the other hand, it breaks up the latent coherences and dynamic patterns of nature, tearing away from it certain features which lend themselves to mechanical organization and manipulation. Immensely brilliant and successful as this has often been in hard operational achievements, it has tended to give rise to what Richard Schlegel has called a 'malevolent technology'.[56] Here we have the creation of mechanisms in which man embodies his own devices, but which have a sinister habit of gaining a momentum of their own and exercising a demonic-like power over man himself, in which the outraged universe seems to be seeking its revenge on him. This applies of course not only to the mechanical machinery devised by technology but to its conceptual 'machinery', the instrumentalist modes of thought created through splitting off symbol from reality or abstracting form from material content in order to extend the power and range of our theoretic tools, but too often our thinking is taken over by the very momentum of their operation, so that it is carried past or beyond the realities we are investigating or is tempted to impose on them a frame of interpretation and explanation that is only partially appropriate. These conceptual instruments are essential to science and their creation represents some of the most brilliant achievements of the human mind; there is nothing wrong or disorderly about them as such, even though they suspend the natural relation between symbol and reality or form and content. They do have, however, a specialist and restricted function to perform, so that everything depends on the way they are used—or misused, for they can become the instruments of disorder.

Disorder arises when abstractive methods and concepts are extended beyond their restricted context or purpose in order to yield generalizations held to be compellingly valid, and thereby give rise to damaging artificiality and misconception in conflict with the natural coherence and order of things. This is the danger of what James Clerk Maxwell called 'partial explanation', for example, a mechanical explanation of the electromagnetic field which is true only up to a point but which is ultimately 'unworkable'.[57] The problem does not lie in the fact that a scientific theory may be true and may work up to a point—which of course applies to all theories—but in a failure to recognize it as a partial explanation and therefore in giving it a completeness which makes it clash with what Heisenberg liked to call 'the central order'. Partial explanations or 'partial orders' which are no longer directed toward a unifying centre can clash, Heisenberg pointed out, and the result is the very opposite of order. Hence he could speak of partial order that has split away from the central order and does not fit into it as a demon let loose and doing a lot of mischief.[58] That is the kind of subtle evil that we frequently come across in the technological as well as the moral domain, when a half-explanation or a half-truth invested with scientific sanction causes deep disorder. It is malevolent and disorderly precisely in so far as it is clothed with a measure of rightness.

Beneath all this, however, there appears to be another problem, in the 'fallen' nature of humanity. That is to say, we have to reckon with a deep split in man himself when he breaks loose from a proper interaction with his Creator and therefore from the ultimate ordering of his rationality from above. This split is manifested not only in the gap that has opened up between what he is and what he ought to be but in a schizoid state of affairs in his inward and his outward relations, and therefore in the operation of his reason as well as in the behaviour of his personality. If man's function in the inter-level connections of nature is to serve their coherent order and harmony, enabling different levels of reality to define and express their rationality through his interaction with them, then any disorder in himself will inevitably be reflected in the way he handles, interprets, and explains the orderly structures of nature of which he constitutes an integral, and indeed an integrating, factor. There is a complex mutual and not a simple linear relation between the order within man and the order within his environment, for they affect one another. Hence as E.H. Hutten has remarked: 'External order and regularity and reality can be recognized only if we have brought order into our inner chaos, and inner order can be established only through experiencing the order of the external world'.[59]

There is rather more to the problem than this, for man and nature do not build together some kind of closed equilibrium system. Certainly, as was suggested earlier, interaction with the objective order of the universe around him has a rectifying and remedial effect on man, evident, for example, in the kind of sanctity or integrity of conscience that is the fruit of rigorous scientific fidelity to the intrinsic rationalities of the real world. However, since the data with which he operates result from his scientific interaction with nature, man cannot shut his eyes to the fact that he himself is an inevitable coefficient in all his relations with nature, in all the questions he puts to nature and in all his deciphering and formulation of the answers nature gives him. Hence it is man himself who needs to be put in the right both with God and with the creation if there is to be an adequate and truthful matching of the order within him and the order outside of him, otherwise his way of ordering the natural world may have the effect of compounding any disorder latent in it. This is why 'scientifically' created disorder in the ecological chaos of nature or of human society can be so sinister and demonic in character. Man himself needs to be redeemed, put right with God, and saved from his diseased self-reference which alienates him from the rest of creation, if he himself is to fulfil a redemptive function in nature, saving it from pointlessness and disorder and mediating to it meaning and harmony from the Creator. It is because the deliverance of the natural order from subjection to futility and corruption ultimately depends on the destiny of man in his relation to God the Father, that St. Paul could speak of all creation as if it were in the agony of travail waiting for God to restore man to sonship and to redeem even his physical existence. That is surely, in part at least, the relevance of the Christian message for natural science as well as for theology.

At an earlier juncture in our discussion we paused to consider God's decisive rejection of evil and his victory over it through the passion and resurrection of Jesus Christ his incarnate Son, in order to derive from it by way of implication a realist assessment of the fearful enormity and malevolent actuality of evil, which we are not in a position to do otherwise, both because evil represents a breach in ontological and rational continuity and because we ourselves are so deeply implicated in it as 'fallen' creatures. Now we return to consider God's action in Christ in a more direct way in order to grasp something of the positive significance of his salvation and redemption of man at the very heart of the creation.

This time we begin with the incarnation, an utterly astonishing event, which would be quite unthinkable except on the ground its actual happening has established: the coming of God himself into the universe he had created. Of course God never was absent from it, for he unceasingly enfolds it in the ontological embrace of his creative presence—otherwise it would slip away altogether into non-existence. The incarnation means that God has made himself present within his creation in an entirely new way, in that the eternal Word of God, the personal mode and activity of his being, by whom the universe was created and from whom it received its order and in whom it consists, has himself become man in Jesus Christ, in whom he makes our creaturely existence his own. The purpose of the incarnation, revealed above all in the passion and resurrection of Christ, was to penetrate into the innermost centre of our contingent existence, in its finite, fragile, and disrupted condition, in order to deliver it from the evil to which it had become subjected, healing and re-ordering it from its ontological roots and entirely renewing its relation to the Creator. That is not something that creatures could in any way do for themselves, for any resistance to evil they might be able to offer or any apparent self-restoration they might be able to achieve could not offset the fact that they themselves have become evil, so that all they do partakes of what they are, any more than a plus sign within the brackets of a mathematical equation could offset a minus sign set in front of them. Effectively to resist evil or to renew itself, the creature would have to repeat the act of creation itself, but only God can do that. And so God himself became a creature in order to do for the creature what the creature could in no way do for itself.

The incarnation is to be interpreted as the alliance of the Creator with his creation in actualization of his will to make himself responsible for its preservation and salvation. In and through the incarnation of his beloved Son God has laid hold of man in his contingence and in his disorder in order to make good his support of man's fleeting, evanescent creatureliness and rectify its internal disruption. Thus understood, the birth, life, passion, and resurrection of Jesus Christ are continuous and indivisible in the redemptive movement of God's love. The only contingence we actually know is a disordered contingence, so that the work of the incarnation within it is at once a creative re-ordering of our existence in which the passion and resurrection of Jesus Christ play an absolutely essential and climactic part. Thus the incarnation represents the almighty condescension and self-humiliation of the Son of God to be one with us in our contingent being in which we are menaced by nothingness—this is the import of the Pauline concept of *kenosis*—and where we have rebelled against our dependence on the Creator and sought to make ourselves autonomous only to find ourselves trapped in our brokenness, all in order to forge an unbreakable ontological bond of love between the creature and the Creator in Jesus Christ.[60] He is the one Mediator between man and God, the man in whom human and divine natures are indissolubly united, and through whom the created order is preserved and secured in such a way that it can no more disintegrate and disappear than the incarnation, passion, and resurrection of Jesus Christ can be undone.

Regarded intensively, the incarnation is the propitiatory movement of God's holy love in human being, reconciling man with God and therein healing the deep split within man himself, unifying his inner and outer life or his spiritual and physical existence, but also reconciling man with his neighbour and with the rest of creation. Hence through Jesus Christ there takes place a restoration of man's proper interaction both with the Creator and with the creation, for in Christ a creative centre of healing and integration has been set up within the structure and density of human contingent being, which cannot but affect the whole created order with which man has to do.

Essential to all this is the vicarious and atoning activity of God's love in the life of Jesus Christ which moved to its culmination in his crucifixion and resurrection. In fulfilment of the divine purpose of salvation the incarnation of God in our world involved such an entry into our fallen and lost condition that God placed himself under the power of evil in order to break it, and took our pain and hurt and suffering into himself in order to quench them in his divine serenity, thus bringing peace to his creation. This movement of God's holy love into the heart of the world's evil and agony is not to be understood as a direct act of sheer almighty power, for it is not God's purpose to shatter and annihilate the agents and embodiments of evil in the world, but rather to pierce into the innermost centre of evil power where it is entrenched in the piled-up and self-compounding guilt of humanity in order to vanquish it from within and below, by depriving it of the lying structures of half-truth on which it thrives and of the twisted forms of legality behind which it embattles itself and from which it fraudulently gains its power. Here we have an entirely different kind and quality of power, for which we have no analogies in our experience to help us understand it, since it transcends every kind of moral and material power we know, the power which the Bible calls *grace*, the incredible power which can undo sin, cancel out wicked deeds, wipe away shameful stains and fearful wounds inflicted on human existence, power which can abrogate guilt, unmake and repair the past, and set everything on an entirely new basis. Such is the grace of the Lord Jesus Christ manifested both in his crucifixion and in his resurrection, and it is still in that form of grace that the power of God meets our life in forgiveness and renewal.

The awesome profundity of this expiatory and propitiatory work of grace in Jesus Christ baffles our comprehension. The road that God took to the Cross through his incarnate alliance with us means that his work of grace took place within the conditions of our alienated existence which is not only subject to the destructive negation of evil but also subject to the divine judgement in its unmitigated negation of evil. That is the fearful state of affairs that makes the Cross with its cry of dereliction so indescribably terrible, for it is the sheer anguish of God (who had, as it were, staked his own being for our salvation) bowed under his own final judgement upon sin in our human existence. The immeasureable significance of the atonement lays hold of us in the realization that this was not the work of an intermediary but of *God himself*, whose action and whose being are one. However, this work of God in the incarnate life, crucifixion, and resurrection of Christ is not one that is forcibly imposed upon man from above and from outside, but a work of God incarnate issuing from below and from within man. While it is irreducibly the work of God in his saving penetration into the ontological depths of human being, it is nevertheless the work of God *as man*, translated into and rising out of human being as genuinely the work of man. On the one hand, it is the act of God in his unconditional love creatively restoring and re-ordering man's existence, while judging and rejecting rebellion and disorder. On the other hand, it is the act of man in love toward God and in obedient acceptance of his will, while judging and rejecting human self-will and disobedience. While doubtless we must think of it in this dual way both from the side of God toward man and from the side of man toward God, the reconciling act of God in Jesus Christ is indivisibly one in the unity of his Person. He is the Mediator between God and man and between man and God who constitutes in himself the divine-human bridge across the chasm of alienation, disruption, and death, and opens the way through his resurrection into a new state of affairs far transcending the old, in which evil and disorder will be finally eliminated and God's purpose of love for his creation will be perfectly fulfilled.

According to the Christian gospel, then, it is in the grace of our Lord Jesus Christ actualized through his crucifixion and resurrection that God has given his ultimate answer to the question of evil in the creation, for therein he manifests in redemption the unique power by which he created the universe and by which he triumphs over all the forces of disintegration and disorder in the cosmos. Yet this is only at the cost of an act, utterly incomprehensible to us, whereby God has taken the sorrow, pain, and agony of the universe into himself in order to resolve it all through his own eternal righteousness, tranquillity, and peace. The centre and heart of that incredible movement of God's love is located in the Cross of Christ, for there we learn that God has refused to hold himself aloof from the violence and suffering of his creatures, but has absorbed and vanquished them in himself, while the resurrection tells us that the outcome of that is so completely successful in victory over decay, decomposition, and death, that all creation with which God allied himself so inextricably in the incarnation has been set on the entirely new basis of his saving grace.

In order to indicate the relevance of this for our present discussion, we may lay stress on three significant points.

1. The fact that God has taken the way of becoming man in allying himself with contingent existence and thereby effecting the redemption of the creation from within its ontological foundations, immensely reinforces the unique place of man in the universe. And in that it is redeemed man who is established at the head of the whole system of inter-level interaction throughout the created order, man's priestly function in the universe now takes on the pattern of a redemptive mission to nature. It is in this light that Christian theology must regard man's God-given role in natural scientific inquiry, that is, not only to be the constituent element in the universe whereby it unfolds and expresses its inherent rational order, but to be the instrument under God whereby physical evil and disorder are rectified and are made, contrary to what they may actually be, to serve the whole created order. However it is only as man himself is healed of his own inward split and disorder that he may exercize a truly integrative and re-ordering role in the world around him.

2. The fact that in his answer to the challenge of evil God's redemptive purpose has been actualized through the incarnate life, passion, and resurrection of Jesus, within the space-time structure of our world, means that physical and material

reality fall within the range of that divine purpose. From the perspective of what God has done for man in the body and blood of Christ, we cannot isolate the evil in which man himself has become entangled from his participation in the structure of the natural order, nor can we segregate the redemption of man from his own evil condition in sin and guilt from the redemption of the whole physical and natural order from the evil to which it has been subjected. The Cross of Christ tells us unmistakably that all physical evil, not only pain, suffering, disease, corruption, death, and of course cruelty and venom in animal as well as human behaviour, but also 'natural' calamities, devastations, and monstrosities, are an outrage against the love of God and a contradiction of good order in his creation. This does not allow us to regard evil and disorder in the universe as in any way intended or as given a direct function by God in the development of his creation, although it does mean that even these enormities can be made by God's incredible power to serve his final end for the created order, much as he has made the dastardly violence of men in crucifying Jesus to serve his healing purpose for mankind, without in any way justifying our human evil and guilt that brought Jesus to the Cross.[61] How the love of God can thus make all things to work together for good is quite beyond our powers of comprehension or imagination, but what we may do, and this is laid upon us as Christians, is to let the Cross and resurrection of Christ be the fixed point by reference to which we may chart in our understanding and expectation the fulfilment of God's redemptive will for the whole creation.

3. The fact that God's redemption and renewal of the creation involved the incarnation or embodiment in it of his own personal mode of being and action as *Word*, from whom the universe received its being and order and by which it is ceaselessly sustained, means that the ontological relation between the contingent universe and the Creator is securely anchored in God himself. The damaging refraction introduced by evil into its contingent relation to God is repaired so that contingence from God and contingence on God may once more be interlocked. Contingent existence is finite, limited at its beginning and limited at its end, and as such in its spatial and temporal extension and restriction is open to

mathematical calculation and description. The form of its physical or empirical existence is subject to *number*,[62] the mode of rational order which makes it accessible to natural scientific analysis, computation, and explanation. However, when the relation between the contingent universe and the Creator is damaged, contingent reality, above all in our interaction with it, tends to resile from its creative and ordering source and to close in autonomously upon itself. In this state of affairs, as we have seen, the universe appears ambiguous and opaque to us, so that the Creator is obscured from our view, for the reference of intelligibility immanent in nature breaks away and bends back on itself, like a spent arrow falling back to the earth. Hence it is the constant temptation of man in the universe to think of it as a self-existing, self-containing, self-ordering, and self-explaining system. In this event he is inclined to abstract and idealize its immanent mathematical relations and even to objectify them, and thereby to secure the fleeting contingent realities of cosmic existence in perpetual determinate forms or timeless necessary truths. Of course such an objectification is no more than a mythological projection of fantasies arising out of man's inner schizoid condition and cannot succeed — thus when number is cut off from its empirical ground, mathematics collapses into a meaningless tautological system. All this has the effect of compounding the damaging estrangement of the universe from the Creator through man's inter-action with it, by imposing on it a rigid determinist framework of mathematical and mechanical connections. Theologically speaking, therefore, the conception of a closed mechanistic universe would seem to be the product of what St. Paul called our 'alienation in mind' from God.

This outlook upon the universe and its immanent order, however, is radically called in question by the incarnation of the Word within the spatio-temporal structures and objectivities of contingent existence, for in the incarnation the Creator breaks into the closed autonomy of the world and restores it to the theonomy of its creative source. Through the Word our self-contained world of idealized mathematical connections is opened out and correlated once more both to its ultimate ground and reason in the transcendent rationality of God and to its proximate ground and reason in the immanent rationality of contingent and empirical reality. Through the Word addressed by God to us in Jesus Christ summoning us to respond to him with the whole of our rational and physical being, we are reminded that 'number' is not an independent mode of rationality but obtains only along with 'word',[63] our other primary mode of rationality, and that they are conjoint forms of contingent order deriving from and pointing to the non-contingent, self-sufficient order beyond them in God. Thus an epistemological as well as an ontological effect of the incarnation of the Word, from whom our word and number rationalities in the created order derive, is to disclose and re-establish the all-important connection between number and word in our human interaction with the rest of the creation. That is an essential part of God's redemptive renewal of the contingent order. On the one hand, it heals the disorderly break between word and number that has opened up in our understanding of the universe and its contingent order, which is nowhere more evident than in the unhappy cultural split between the humanities and the sciences. Thereby, however, there has been opened up for us a way forward in the integration of human knowledge and culture. On the other hand, in coordinating the modalities and functions of number and word, God's redemptive renewal of the contingent order also heals the disorderly break in the semantic reference of the universe beyond itself and thereby restores to the universe its lost meaning. Hence as the orderly structures and laws of nature become more and more disclosed to our scientific inquiry, far from proving to be meaningless, they are found to be replete with significance in that through their connection with word they are enabled to witness to God, the creative source of their rationality. It may indeed be claimed that under the creative impact of the incarnate Word of God the contingent order of the universe constitutes a sort of sounding-board which echoes and resonates God's Word in such a way that the universe praises and glorifies its Creator and Redeemer.

A prayer of James Clerk Maxwell found among his papers:

'O Lord, our Lord, how excellent is Thy name in all the earth, who has set thy glory above the heavens, and out of the mouths of babes and sucklings hast perfected praise. When we consider Thy heavens and the work of Thy fingers, the moon and the stars which Thou hast ordained, teach us to know that Thou art mindful of us, and visitest us, making us rulers over the works of Thy hands, showing us the wisdom of Thy laws, and crowning us with honour and glory in our earthly life; and looking higher than the heavens, may we see Jesus, made a little lower than the angels for the suffering of death, crowned with glory and honour, that He, by the grace of God, should taste death for every man. O Lord, fulfil Thy promise, and put all things in subjection under His feet. Let sin be rooted out from the earth, and let the wicked be no more. Bless thou the Lord, O my soul, praise the Lord.'

Notes

Chapter 1

1. See my discussion in *Space, Time, and Incarnation* (1969), and below, pp. 12 f., 38 f.
2. Cf. S.L. Jaki, *Science and Creation: From Eternal Cycles to an Oscillating Universe* (1974).
3. See below, pp. 39 f, 73 f., 109 f.; and also G. Florovsky, *Creation and Redemption, Collected Works*, vol. iii (1976), pp. 43-78.
4. *Space, Time, and Incarnation*, p. 75.
5. See further, *Theology in Reconciliation* (1975), pp. 220 f, 226 f.
6. Sir Isaac Newton, *Principia*, Cajori edit. (republished 1966), pp. xxxi f. 544, 546 f; *Opticks*, 4th edn., 1730 (republished 1952), p. 369; and *Principia*, pp. xxvii, xxxif, 545 f; *Opticks*, p. 403; *Letters to Richard Bentley* (*Newton's Philosophy of Nature. Selections from his Writings*, by H.S. Thayer, 1953), pp. 47 ff., 53, 57 f., 65 ff.
7. *Opticks*, pp. 352 f, 402 f; *Principia*, pp. 543 f, 546; *Letters to Richard Bentley*, pp. 48 f, 52 f, 55 ff.
8. P.S. Laplace, *Méchanique céleste* (1799), xv, p. 324.
9. Cf. *Principia*, p. xxxii; *Opticks*, pp. 370, 402, and see above, 6. See also Cotes' 'Preface to the Second Edition', *Principia*, pp. xxvii ff.
10. A. Einstein, *The World as I See It* (1935), p. 148.
11. Cf. Newton's preface to the first edition of the *Principia*: 'The solution of these problems is required from mechanics, and by geometry the use of them, when so solved, is shown.' p. xvii. This is very apparent in Newton's equation of the laws of motion with 'axioms' in the classical sense, *Principia*, p. 13 f. However, the fact that Newton was not able completely to recast all fluxions (the even flowing of a continuous function) into this axiomatic form, would seem to indicate that his fluxions were more flexible than idealized geometrical relations.
12. See the important paper by A.H. Cook on 'Standards of Measurement and the Structure of Physical Knowledge', in which he shows that even when we adopt a realist position, as he does, we have to recognize that 'the standards of measurement employed in physics are arbitrary' *Contemporary Physics* (1977), vol. xviii, no. 4, pp. 393-409. This warns us to beware of confusing the actual state of the physical world with the measurements we make of it, notwithstanding the fact that the choice of standards is made under the constraint of a physical world existing independently of our observations and measurements.
13. Max Born, *The Born-Einstein Letters* (1971), pp. 221 ff.

14. See Einstein and Infeld, *The Evolution of Physics* (1938), p. 193, and William Berkson, *Fields of Force* (1974), pp. 309-12.
15. David Bohm, *Causality and Chance in Modern Physics*, Harper edit. (1961), p. 86.
16. Einstein and Infeld, op. cit., p. 244.
17. Cf. W.P. Carvin, 'Leibniz on Motion and Creation', *Journal of the History of Ideas*, vol. xxxiii, no. 3 (1972), pp. 425-38.
18. Michael Polanyi, *Scientific Thought and Social Reality*, ed. F. Schwarz (1974), p. 136f.
19. This notion of 'differentiality' is borrowed from engineering science rather than from mathematics.

Chapter 2

1. The idea that knowledge of nature cannot be gained through the reason alone became established through the work of Galileo, Bacon, and Newton, in two stages: in rejection of the essentialist approach to scientific knowledge advocated by the ancient and mediaeval worlds, and in rejection of the rationalism of Descartes, Spinoza, and Leibniz. After a throwback in the nineteenth century, e.g. in J. Tyndall, *Fragments of Science* (1901), Einstein finally established that the basic concepts and laws of science cannot be deduced from material experience by logical methods. See 'The Principles of Scientific Research', *The World as I See It*, pp. 123 ff., and further my paper, 'The Integration of Form in Natural and in Theological Science', *Science, Medicine and Man*, vol. i (1973), pp. 143-72; and Gerald Holton, 'The Mainsprings of Discovery — The Great Tradition', *Science* (April 1974), pp. 85-92.
2. See the excellent little book by Alastair McKinnon, *Falsification and Belief* (1970), pp. 18, 28ff.
3. Cf. E.L. Mascall, *Christian Theology and Natural Science* (1957), pp. 98ff, 104ff, 110ff, 125ff.
4. See J.W.N. Watkins, 'Between Analytic and Empirical', *Philosophy* (1957), pp. 112-31; 'Confirmable and Influential Metaphysics', *Mind* (1958), pp. 344-65; 'When are Statements Empirical?', *The British Journal for the Philosophy of Science* (1960), pp. 287-308.
5. I have in mind here the point made by Leibniz that necessary and contingent truths differ as rational numbers and surds, and that in the case of surds, reduction involves an infinite process, and yet approaches a common measure, so that a definite but unending series is obtained. Thus contingent truths require an infinite analysis, which God alone can accomplish. *Die philosophischen Schriften von G.W. Leibniz*, ed. C.J. Gerhardt (1875-90), vol. v, p. 268; vol. vii, p. 200. See Bertrand Russell, *A Critical Exposition of the Philosophy of Leibniz* (1900), p. 60f.
6. Cf. J.A. Wheeler: 'Expansion and later attainment of a maximum volume, according to Einstein's theory, are the prelude to contraction and complete collapse. Collapse confronts us with what, in

my view, is the greatest crisis in the history of physics, because in it we hear physics apparently saying that physics must come to an end... Well-established and never-contradicted theory tells us that a time must arrive when physical law ends: there is no law of physics that does not demand space and time for its statement. With the collapse of space, and the end of time, the very framework for every law of physics therefore also collapses.' 'The Universe as Home for Man', *American Scientist*, vol. lxi, no. 6 (November–December 1974), p. 686. See also J.A. Wheeler, 'From relativity to mutability', in J. Mehra, (ed.) *The Physicist's Conception of Nature* (1973), pp. 202–47.

7. Cf. J.A. Wheeler, again: 'The so-called "big numbers" ($\sim 10^{80}$ particles in the universe; $\sim 10^{40}$ of radius of universe at maximum expansion to effective size of an elementary particle; $\sim 10^{40}$ ratio between elementary particle dimensions and the Planck length) have never received a physical explanation. They never will, if they are initial value data! Physics can unravel dynamic law, but it has never found what principle fixes the other half of dynamics, the "initial conditions" of nature.' ('From Mendeleev's Atom to the Collapsing Star', Estratto dagli Atti del Convegno Mendeleeviano, *Accademia delle Scienze di Torino — Accademia Nazionale dei Lincei* (Sept. 1969), p. 226f).

8. This point is frequently made by Richard Feynman, since science must propose laws beyond their observed range if it is to avoid simply describing experiments. 'We must always make statements about the regions we have not seen, or the whole business is of no use.' *The Character of Physical Law* (1965), p.76; cf. also pp. 50 f, 67 f, 76, 94, 162. This was Polanyi's emphasis at the opening of his discussion in *Personal Knowledge*, (1958): 'In this wholly indeterminate scope of its true implications lies the deepest sense in which objectivity is attributed to a scientific theory.' (p. 5).

9. The example of general relativity is of especial significance for our purpose since through it the universe is defined as a whole — 'finite yet unbounded', as Einstein expressed it, *Ideas and Opinions* (1954), p. 240.

10. A. Einstein, 'The Method of Theoretical Physics', *Ideas and Opinions*, p. 275.

11. See H. Diels, *Die Fragmente der Vorsokratiker* (ed. W. Kranz, 1954), Fragments A and B. Greek thought frequently drew a distinction between *ouk on* = non-being in the sense of 'blank nothing', and *me on* = non-being in the sense of an antithetical form of being or negative being. Thus Aristotle could relate the antithesis between being and non-being to hot and cold (*Metaphysics* A 986 b). Generally, however, while *ouk on* was used to refer to sheer nothingness, *me on* was used to refer to irrational, defective, disorderly being.

12. For a very helpful analysis of Greek conceptions of God and nature, the Greek conception of science as operating *more geometrico*, and the 'un-Greek' elements needed for the rise of empiri-

cal science, see the articles by M.B. Foster in *Mind*, vol. xliii, no. 171 (1934), pp. 446–68; vol. xliv, no. 176 (1935), pp. 439–66; vol. xlv, no. 177 (1936), pp. 1–27. While Foster shows the essential place of contingence in the rise of empirical science, he does not focus attention on contingent order or intelligibility, nor does he deal with the all-important patristic roots of these notions. See also John Baillie, *Natural Science and the Spiritual Life, Being the Philosophical Discourse delivered before the British Association for the Advancement of Science at Edinburgh, on 12 August 1951*, in which he relates the rise of empirical science to the rejection of the Aristotelian notion of final causes (pp. 16 ff).

13. Cf. A. Ehrhardt, *The Beginning. A Study in the Greek Philosophical Approach to the Concept of Creation from Anaximander to St. John* (1968). Particularly instructive is Plato's *Sophistes-Politicus* in which the idea is entertained that God creates all real things without any pre-existing material (265c); but it is clear that the Greeks found it impossible to regard thinking or speaking of nothing as other than implying *something*, as if nothing were some sort of material, and as having a form of existence like being, (257b–258e). Thus also Democritus, 'the nothing exists as much as the thing', in Diels, *Die Fragmente de Vorsokratiker*, Fragment B. Cf. the critique of this notion by the Christian physicist John Philoponos of Alexandria in AD517, *Commentary on Aristotle's Physics*, p. 189, ed. H. Vitelli (1887–88). But see especially the superb paper by Georges Florovsky, 'The Idea of Creation in Christian Philosophy', *Creation and Redemption* (*Collected Works*, vol. iii, 1976), pp. 43–78.

14. This is a question as to the absolute necessity of our actual universe including its initial conditions: why is there something and not nothing, and why this particular something?—to which only an *extrinsic* answer can be given, i.e. from divine revelation. It must be distinguished, therefore, from the extremely interesting question behind the so-called 'anthropic principle': given the initial conditions of the universe, why has it expanded in such a way as to give rise to man?—to which an answer may be given in the light of the realization that if the universe were not what it actually is, no intelligent life could have developed and it would not be comprehensible. Cf. J.A. Wheeler, 'The Universe as Home for Man', *American Scientist*, vol. lxii, no. 6 (December 1974), pp. 683–91; and 'Genesis and Observership', *Proceedings* (of the Congress), University of Western Ontario Series in the Philosophy of Science, ed. R. Butts and J. Hintikka (1977); Sir Bernard Lovell, *In the Center of Immensities* (1976), pp. 110 ff, 122 ff; and B.J. Carr and M.J. Rees, 'The Anthropic Principle and the Structure of the Physical World', in *Nature* (April 1979), p. 605, to which Bernard Lovell has drawn my attention.

15. See p. 5.
16. See p. 22 f.
17. This method of testing the compatibility of theory with nature by

means of specially devised experiments Newton spoke of as keeping to 'the analogy of nature' (*Principia*, p.398f). It sometimes arises, however, as Richard Feynman has pointed out, that more than one theory may agree with experiment to the same extent, so that other grounds for choosing one instead of another must be adopted (*The Character of Physical Law*, pp.50ff, 168f). In these circumstances doubtless the criterion of beauty will be decisive, in the conviction that nature has a simplicity and therefore a great beauty (p.173). Einstein laid the emphasis here on what he called 'inner perfection' as well as 'external confirmation', 'logical simplicity' as well as 'naturalness'. P.A. Schilpp, 'Autobiographical Notes', *Albert Einstein:Philosopher-Scientist*, pp.23, 29, 33, etc.

18. E.L. Mascall, *Christian Theology and Natural Science*, p.97.
19. Ibid., p.104. Cf. also M.K. Munitz, *Space, Time and Creation* (1957), pp.78ff.
20. A. Einstein, 'Principles of Scientific Research', *The World as I See It*, p.125.
21. A. Einstein, 'The Method of Theoretical Physics', *The World as I See It*, p.136; 'The Problem of Space, Ether, and the Field in Physics', p.173.
22. A. Einstein, 'The Fundaments of Theoretical Physics', *Ideas and Opinions*, pp.323ff.; 'Physics and Reality', pp.290ff.
23. A. Einstein, 'The Problem of Space, Ether and the Field in Physics', *The World as I See It*, p.180.
24. E.L. Mascall, *Christian Theology*, pp.110ff, 117ff. Einstein himself objected to the removal of certain fundamental concepts from the domain of empiricism: *The Meaning of Relativity* (1923), p.2 f.
25. Isaac Newton, *Principia*, p.192. Cf. also p.xvii f, and *Opticks*, pp.404ff.
26. J.D. Bernal, *Science in History*, vol.ii, *The Scientific and Social Revolutions* (1954), p.487.
27. *Principia*, p.547; *Opticks*, p.369. Cf. also *Principia*, p.550, and the fourth rule of reasoning, p.400; and Newton's letter to Cotes in H.S. Thayer, *Newton's Philosophy of Nature. Selections from his Writings*, p.7.
28. See above, pp.92 ff.
29. I. Kant, *Metaphysische Anfangsgründe der Naturwissenschaft*: 'Our intellect does not draw its laws from nature, but imposes its laws upon nature.' Cited from Sir Karl Popper, *Conjectures and Refutations: The Growth of Scientific Knowledge* (1963), pp.48, 180. See also Kant, *Critique of Pure Reason*, A 126, 127.
30. Kant, *Critique of Pure Reason*, B 289-290; A 766=B 794.
31. Max Born, *The Born-Einstein Letters*, letters 115-116, pp.221-8.
32. Ibid., pp.221ff., 225f. See above p.13.
33. *The World as I See It*, p.135f.
34. For these oracular sayings of Einstein, see Born, *The Born-Einstein Letters*, pp.149, 199; F.S.C. Northrop, *Man, Nature and God* (1962), p.209f; and J. Bernstein, *Einstein* (1973), p.61.

35. Werner Heisenberg, *Physics and Beyond* (1971), p. 237 ff.

36. Ibid., p. 243.

37. See M. Polanyi, *Personal Knowledge* (1958), pp. 35, 392, ff; *Meaning* (1975), pp. 162 ff.

38. Heisenberg, *Physics and Beyond*, pp. 84, 214 ff, 241, 247.

39. See the enlightening account of Clerk Maxwell's thought by Richard Olson, *Scottish Philosophy and British Physics 1770–1880* (1975), pp. 299 ff.

40. A similar point is made by Polanyi in his argument that a 'Laplacean' representation of relations inherent in nature in terms of exact atomic topography inevitably leaves out of account the all-important dynamic processes and integrating functions in any field of scientific inquiry. See *Personal Knowledge*, pp. 139 ff; *Knowing and Being* (1969), pp. 177 ff; *Meaning*, pp. 29 ff, 142 ff; 'Science and Man', *Proceedings of the Royal Society of Medicine*, vol. lxiii (September 1970), p. 974 f.

41. Ilya Prigogine, 'The Metamorphosis of Science: Culture and Science Today', *Communications of the New York Symposium* (July 1977), Académie Internationale des Science Religieuses et Académie Internationale de Philosophie des Sciences (1978), pp. 159 ff. See also 'Time, Structure and Fluctuations', *Science* (Sept. 1978), vol. cci, no. 4358, pp. 777 ff.

42. See the discussion of this by John Macmurray, *Interpreting the Universe* (1933), pp. 64–83, 84–102.

43. Cf. James Clerk Maxwell's warning against the danger of 'partial explanations', particularly in the use of mechanical models, in *The Scientific Papers of James Clerk Maxwell* ed. W.D. Niven (1890), vol. i, pp. 155 f.

44. W.A. Elsasser, *Atom and Organism* (1966). In spite of the enormous progress in biochemistry and molecular biology in physico-chemical analysis, heterogeneous features in living organisms, which resist formalizations that compound like with like, require some sort of *multivariable organic order* or *open field-structure* — cf. Ludwig van Bertalannffy, *Modern Theories of Development: An Introduction to Theoretical Biology* (1933), and *General System Theory* (1968). Cf. also C.F.A. Pantin, *The Relations between the Sciences* ed. A.M. Pantin and W.H. Thorpe (1968), who proposed the deployment of J.H. Newman's concept of 'illative sense' to help transcend the evident gap between logical analysis and appreciation of organic form.

45. Clearly Newton would have nothing to do with the 'pure mathematics' of the Cartesians, for in the actual world with which Newton was concerned mathematics has to do with physical principles and quantifiable relations. Cf. *Principia*, p. xvii: 'Therefore geometry is founded in mechanical practice, and is nothing but that part of universal mechanics which accurately proposes and demonstrates the art of measuring'. Nevertheless, because Newton brought in the fictitious concepts of absolute time and space which through their unchanging uniformity inertially con-

ditioned the whole mechanical system, in actual fact he offered an account of the universe of bodies in motion through exact mathematical formalization and generalization which appeared to be necessarily true and which artificially imposed an abstract homogeneity upon nature. Yet, as Einstein put it, in the contemporary state of science, this was the only possible and the only fruitful thing to do; see Foreword to Max Jammer, *Concepts of Space* (1960), p. xv. The basic problem, as Polanyi points out, relates to the external bearing of mathematical thinking upon forms inherent in nature (*Personal Knowledge*, p. 8 f).

46. Einstein, *The World as I See It*, pp. 125 f, 133, 135 f, 173 f.
47. Einstein, *Ideas and Opinions*, p. 226.
48. Einstein, *The Meaning of Relativity* (5th edn., 1956), p. 2.
49. Einstein, 'Geometry and Experience', *Ideas and Opinions*, pp. 223, 240.
50. For a fuller account of this see my essay, 'The Integration of Form in Natural and in Theological Science', *Science, Medicine and Man*, vol. i (1973), pp. 143–72. The epistemological implications of general relativity have been admirably worked out in three of the contributions to the volume edited by P.A. Schilpp, *Albert Einstein: Philosopher–Scientist*; 'Einstein's theory of Knowledge', by V.F. Lenzen, pp. 357–84; 'Einstein's Conception of Science', by F.S.C. Northrop, pp. 387–408; and 'Einstein's Theory of Relativity, viewed from the Standpoint of Critical Realism, and its Significance for Philosophy', by Aloys Wenzl, pp. 583–606.
51. S.W. Hawking, 'Black Holes and Unpredictability', *Physics Bulletin* (January 1978), vol. ixxx. 1, pp. 23–4, reprinted from *Annals of the New York Academy of Sciences, Eighth Texas Symposium on Relativistic Astrophysics*.
52. Richard Feynman, *The Character of Physical Law*, p. 33.
53. The American Academy of Sciences, *The Frontiers and Limits of Science*, publication 65 (1977). Weisskopf does not elaborate the point that neutrons and electrons have no 'memory' of their past, but shows that with the nucleus there is a part-record of its history embedded in it—e.g. a gold nucleus, like that of other heavy elements such as silver and lead, discloses on analysis that it was produced during a supernova explosion. Crystals yield more information, and self-reproducing structures most of all. The brain, which is the last step in the self-producing line, contains the history of all its predecessors but also incorporates the history of its contemporaries by communication. So far as the proton is concerned, Feynman claims that it is not a fundamental particle but is made up of simpler elements called quarks. See 'The Structure of the Proton', *Science* (February 1974), vol. clxxxiii, no. 4125, pp. 601 ff.
54. I. Prigogine and A. Babloyantz, 'Thermodynamics of Evolution', *Physics Today*, no. 11 (1972), pp. 23–8; G. Glansdorff and I. Prigogine, *Thermodynamics of Structure, Stability and Fluctuations* (1971); I. Prigogine and G. Nicolis, *Self-Organization in*

Non-Equilibrium Systems (1977); I. Prigogine, 'Time, Structure and Fluctuations', *Science*, vol. cci, no. 4358 (September 1978), pp. 777–85; 'The Metamorphosis of Science: Culture and Science Today', *Abba Salama*, vol. ix (1978), pp. 155–83; *From Being to Becoming* (1979).

55. See H.J. Hamilton, 'A Thermodynamic Theory of the Origin and Hierarchical Evolution of Living Systems', *Zygon* (December 1977), vol. xii, no. 4, pp. 289–335.

56. Cf. Stephen Weinberg, *The First Three Minutes* (1977), pp. 45, ff, 52 ff, 64 ff; Bernard Lovell, *In the Center of Immensities* (1978), pp. 97 ff; Paul Davies, *The Runaway Universe* (1978), p. 31 f. Cf. also the statement by J.A. Wheeler: 'Never out of the equations of general relativity has one been able to find the slightest argument for a 'reexpansion' or a 'cyclic universe' or anything other than an end.' 'Genesis and Observership', *Proceedings* (of the Congress), University of Western Ontario Series in the Philosophy of Science (1977), p. 13 of the essay.

57. V.F. Weisskopf, 'Of Atoms, Mountains, and Stars: A Study in Qualitative Physics', *Science*, vol. clxxxvii, no. 4177 (February, 1975), pp. 605–12.

58. Any scientific judgment as to whether the universe is expanding at a sufficient rate to resist any possible gravitational collapse back into an 'original' dense state would depend on the knowledge, which we do not have, of the mean density of matter in the universe. But *speculation* as to the possibility of an endless series of alternate movements of expansion and collapse, that is, a so-called 'oscillating universe', would have to reckon with a number of questions such as these. Why, for example, is the fossil radiation from the big bang only $2.7°$ K which from the inevitable necessities of a cyclic universe would be arbitrary? Why, if there has been (and will be) endless cycles of collapse and expansion, is the universe not far hotter than it is, as one might expect from the increase in entropy through such infinite processes? What value could we seriously give to the contingent nature of the universe upon which all our physics depends if the ultimate necessitarianism of a cyclic or oscillating universe could have the effect—as indeed it would— of having to necessitate all the processes down the line, making us regard contingence in the impossible Kantian way as only under conditions of necessity? In other words, speculation as to an oscillating universe would imply connections in thought that would destroy the foundations of physics we actually work with, and invalidate all the results on the ground of which we speculate in this way! It is difficult to avoid the idea that there are types of mind which want to get rid of singularities and contingence at any price!

59. This is not, of course, to depreciate logic or logical argumentation, but to be strictly logical about logic, for logic has to do with the interrelations between ideas or statements, not with the relation between ideas or statements and empirical reality, where we have

to reckon with what Einstein called an 'extra-logical' relation—see again 'The Problem of Space, Ether, and the Field in Physics', *The World as I See It*, pp. 173 ff. If there were a logical relation between knowing and what we know there would be a logical way of deriving knowledge and a logical way of verifying it—but the strange notion of logical induction dies hard! Popper and Polanyi have contributed no less than Einstein to destroying that idea.

60. See S.L. Jaki, *The Relevance of Physics* (1966), pp. 127 ff.

61. *Ideas and Opinions*, pp. 36 ff., 40, 41 ff., 49 ff.

Chapter 3

1. Professor Jaki has suggested that cosmology achieves scientific status from the time of Einstein's 1917 essay on 'Cosmological Considerations of the General Theory of Relativity'. See H.A. Lorentz, A. Einstein, H. Minkowski, and H. Weyl, *The Principle of Relativity*, with notes by A. Sommerfeld, (1952 edit.), pp. 175–88. See S.L. Jaki, *The Road of Science and the Ways of God*, p. 189 f.

2. For example, see St. Augustine, *Contra Faustum Manichaeum*, xx, 7.

3. Plato, *Meno*, 80e–86b.

4. St. Augustine, *Retractationes*, 14.4. Cf. 18.2; *De Trinitate*, xii.15.24. This passage is particularly interesting, for in it St. Augustine retracts his earlier agreement with Plato, *Soliloquia* ii.20.35. Cf. Michael Polanyi, who offers a similar solution to Plato's problem in *The Tacit Dimension* (1967), pp. 22, 24.

5. St. Augustine, *De Vera Religione* 30.56.

6. Cf. here the deeply suggestive book by W.A. Whitehouse, *Order, Goodness and Glory* (1960).

7. See above, p. 88.

8. Op cit., p.17.

9. Whitehouse rightly points out that 'if the notion of a temporal beginning were utterly irrelevant to the natural order, the significance of nature as an historical arrangement could hardly persist, except as a subjective illusion'. ibid., p.41.

10. Ibid., p.52: 'The world is preserved in an historical order where what has occurred does not occur again and where enigmatic patterns of developments are unfolding from the past into the future through the decisive moment which is present.' For the same idea see D. Lamont, *Christ and the World of Thought* (1934), chs. V–VII.

11. For the origins of science as a rigorous form of thought one must look to Euclid and Aristotle, that is, to the foundations of geometry and logic. See A.D. Ritchie, *Studies in the History and Methods of the Sciences* (1958), who points to a wider perspective. See also S. Sambursky, *The Physical World of the Greeks* (1956); and Schrödinger, *Nature and the Greeks* (1954).

12. See n. 4 of Ch. 2, p.144.

13. See above, pp.4 f, pp.39 ff.

14. Two instructive examples of this may be taken from the nineteenth century. 1. Kierkegaard showed in his *Philosophical Fragments*, tr. by D. Swenson (1938), how attempts to understand and interpret, 'becoming' constantly tend to convert it into its opposite, some form of *necessity* — which is relevant to the problems of classical science discussed in the previous chapter. 2. Feuerbach showed in *The Essence of Christianity*, tr. by M. Evans (1893), how nineteenth-century ways of thinking of God turned out to be little more than objectifications of man, thus turning theology into anthropology. Both these movements of thought which twist the truth into its very opposite seem to be combined in the Marxist conception of natural science and its application to human society.

15. This is how, for example, Kierkegaard described the rationalist approach to the relation of 'God' to 'becoming' in the incarnation — that is, in terms of our discussion, the relation of the Creator to contingent reality. See *Concluding Unscientific Postscript*, tr. by D. Swenson and W. Lowrie (1941), pp.188f, 192, 394, 512. The way in which Kierkegaard related what he called 'absolute fact' to 'historical fact' against Lessing's disjunction between 'necessary truths of reason' and 'contingent truths of history' (*Lessing's Theological Writings*, ed. H. Chadwick (1956), p.55) indicates how sharply he was opposed to the dualist modes of thought stemming from Galileo, Descartes, and Newton. It was that dualist assumption that made the Christian doctrine of incarnation appear 'paradoxical' and 'absurd' for it rejected a bifurcation between 'absolute fact' and 'historical fact' (*Philosophical Fragments*, pp.83 f.).

16. This is the contradiction that began to come to light with the attempts of Clerk Maxwell to offer a rigorously mechanical account in the Newtonian manner of the electromagnetic field—the point which made such an impression on Einstein (*The World as I See It*, pp.159-61, 177 ff.).

17. 'Maxwell's paper "On Physical lines of Force" is in some ways the most remarkable in our story. In the paper Maxwell invented and worked with a theory which he thought basically untenable, but he produced results among the most fruitful in the history of science.' W. Berkson, *Fields of Force* (1974), p.170.

18. This was Maxwell's paper 'A Dynamical Theory of the Electromagnetic Field', *The Scientific Papers of James Clerk Maxwell*, pp.526. In his subsequent *Treatise on Electricity and Magnetism* (1873), as R. Olson points out in *Scottish Philosophy and British Physics 1850-1880* (1975), p.297, Maxwell alternated between his mechanical and relational theories. See also Berkson, op. cit., pp.172 ff. 'Maxwell had begun with some confidence in the "Cartesian" world picture, in which all the pervasive medium obeys the laws of Newton's mechanics. But he was unable to construct a viable mechanical explanation of the electromagnetic field, and so he separated the equations from the mechanical analogy, and

tried to argue for field theory in spite of the lack of mechanism for the field.' (p. 181) On the other hand Maxwell produced a later work, *An Elementary Treatise on Electricity* (ed. W. Garnett, 1881), in which he attempted a further geometrical account more in accordance with 'On Faraday's Lines of Force' (*Scientific Papers*, vol. i, pp. 156–229). To the very end he insisted on having two ways of looking at things! (cf. *Scientific Papers*, p. 208).

19. The contrast between classical mechanics and the reality of the field as defined by relativity theory is set out by Einstein (with Infeld) in *The Evolution of Physics from Early Concepts to Relativity and Quanta* (1938). While there are undoubtedly close parallels between Newtonian and Relativistic formulations such that their practical results agree very closely, there is a basic difference between their mechanical and relational nature and framework which is all-important. It was 'contradictions and inconsistencies' in the former which brought about the new concept of the field with its equation of matter and energy and the fusion of space and time (cf. p. 244).

20. Cf. Berkson's illuminating discussion of 'Faraday versus Einstein' in this respect, for Faraday seems to occupy the middle ground in the relation between the Newtonian and Einsteinian views (Op. cit., pp. 323 ff).

21. David Bohm, *Foundation of Physics*, vol. i, no. 4 (1971), pp. 359–81; vol. iii, no. 2 (1973), pp. 139–68.

Chapter 4

1. Cf. St. Thomas Aquinas, *De Aeternitate Mundi contra Murmurantes*, Opusculum IV; cf. his *Summa Theologiae* Ia, q. 19, a.8.

2. St. Thomas, *In Libros Perihermeneias Expositio*, 1, 14.

3. St. Thomas, *Summa Theologiae*, Ia, q.2, a.3; q.86, a.3. Cf. Hans Meyer, *The Philosophy of St. Thomas Aquinas* (1946), pp. 106, 328.

4. In this way contingence is treated by the reason in much the same way as evil, in that 'it cannot be known simply as evil, for its core is hollow, and can be neither recognised nor defined save in terms of the surrounding good'. St. Thomas, *Summa Theologiae*, Ia, q.14.10, a.4. Cf. *De Veritate*, 2.3. See also *De Natura Accidentis*, Opusculum LIV, 1-2.

5. Duns Scotus insisted that all relations between God and his creatures are free and contingent, for they depend entirely on the divine will and being for what they are. In creating the world out of nothing God freely brings new ideas and realities into existence, *De Spiritualitate et Immortalitate Animae Humanae*, I.2.4; *Quodlibetales*, q.15. In this event Scotus rejects the traditional dialectical relation between contingence and necessity, *De Metaphysica*, I.4; *Ordinatio*, d.II, q.1, a.2.

6. Cf. William of Ockham, *Super Sententiis*, I.d.2, q.4.m: 'We know

only propositions, and any science, real or rational, deals exclusively with propositions as such.'

7. St. Thomas, *Compendium Theologiae*, Opusculum XIII, 116-119; *Summa Theologiae*, Ia, 1.49, a.1; *De Malo*, 1, *Quaest. Disp.* II.

8. St. Thomas, *De Substantiis Separatis*, 15-18; *Summa Theologiae*, Ia, q.48, a.5; *Summa contra Gentes*, III.140.

9. St. Thomas, *In Librum VII Metaphysicorum*, 2-3; *In Librum I Physicorum*, 9; *Summa Theologiae*, Ia, q.66, a.2; cf. H. Meyer, op. cit., p. 311 f.

10. St. Thomas, *Summa Theologiae*, Ia, q.49, a.1-2.

11. St. Thomas, *Summa Theologiae*, Ia, q.48, a.1; q.49, a.3; *Compendium Theologiae*, 142.

12. St. Thomas, *De Substantiis Separatis*, 18; *Compendium Theologiae*, 119; cf. Hans Meyer, op.cit., p. 311 f., 382 f.

13. Polanyi, *The Logic of Liberty* (1951), p. 106; *Personal Knowledge* (1958), pp. 231 ff; *Knowing and Being* (1969), pp. 14, 16 ff, 21 f, 44 f; *Meaning* (1975), pp. 18, 28, 63, 213; *Scientific Thought and Social Reality* (1974), pp. 40 ff, 118, 146 ff, etc.

14. An outstanding example of this way of thinking is found in Charles Darwin, *The Origin of Species* (1859), in which change through natural selection is explained in terms of causal mechanisms functioning through all chance mutational events. Here we have manifest a way of thinking that goes back to Laplace, *Exposition du système du monde* (1798), and *Essai philosophique sur les probabilités* (1814), that is, to the idea that every event is causally conditioned in every respect by the totality of circumstances at the moment when it happens. Cf. L. Kolakowski, *The Main Currents of Marxism*, vol. i (1978), p. 385 f. Contrast the celebrated work of Jacques Monod, *Chance and Necessity* (1972), in which sheer randomness is contrasted with necessity in the process of natural selection, but since randomness is geared into the necessity of the consequences of purely chance events it does not appear to be ultimately different from the old dialectic of the accidental and the necessary, in spite of the fact that chance is now given the status of a dogmatic metaphysical idea!

15. Cf. H. Butterfield, *The Origins of Modern Science* (1957); R. Hooykaas, *Religion and the Rise of Modern Science* (1972).

16. Cf. E.A. Burtt, *The Metaphysical Foundations of Modern Science* (3rd edn., 1932), pp. 72 ff, 84 f. For an appreciation of Galileo's rôle here see Einstein and Infeld, *The Evolution of Physics* (1938), p. 6 f, and Einstein's Foreword to Stillman Drake's edition of Galileo, *Dialogue Concerning the Two Chief World Systems* (1967), pp. vii–xix.

17. See Gerd Buchdahl, *Metaphysics and the Philosophy of Science* (1969), pp. 509 ff, 552 ff. F.A. Hayek prefers to trace this constructivism back to Descartes (see *Law, Legislation and Liberty*, vol.i (1973), pp. 8-34) and shows that it regularly led to a revolt against reason, p. 31 f. For the latter see also his *The Counter-Revolution of Science: Studies in The Abuse of Reason* (1952).

18. See Ernst Mach's discussion of 'the economy of science' in *The Science of Mechanics* (1902), pp. 481-94: 'There is no cause nor effect in nature: nature has but an individual existence; nature simply *is*'. (p. 483).

19. David Hume, *A Treatise of Human Nature*, I.xiv; *Enquiries concerning the Human Understanding and concerning the Principles of Morals*, I.vii, 1-2.

20. See N. Kemp Smith, *The Philosophy of David Hume* (1941), pp. 391 f, 411 ff.

21. Hume, *A Treatise of Human Nature*, III.xiv, p. 167 (ed. L. Selby-Bigge).

22. See L. Kolakowski, *The Alienation of Reason* (1968), pp. 36 ff.

23. Hume, *A Treatise of Human Nature*, IV.1, p. 180.

24. E. Mach, *The Science of Mechanics*, p. 582.

25. Ibid., p. 483. Another term he used was 'mental artifice', pp. 492 f.

26. Willard Van Orman Quine, *Word and Object* (1960), pp. 176 ff.

27. E.L. Mascall, *Christian Theology and Natural Science* p. 76.

28. Mach, op. cit., p. 492 f.

29. See S.L. Jaki, *The Relevance of Physics*, pp. 163 f., and pp. 550 f. where he offers full documentation for Mach's contemptuous dismissal of atoms as 'things of thought' and then for his basic change when he came to believe in atoms. Professor Jaki points out that not only J.B. Stallo and W. Oswald, but also F. Nietzsche, took up the same attitude toward 'hypothetical atoms'. See also Jaki's discussion of this in *Science and Creation* (1974), p. 325 f. For a discussion of the relation of Mach's thought to that of Planck, see Jaki's Gifford Lectures, *The Road of Science and the Ways of God* (1978), pp. 174, 176 ff.

30. Einstein's own mind early underwent a deep change toward a full realist position, which is not unconnected with his relation to the thought of Mach. See again Jaki's Gifford Lectures, pp. 181 ff.

31. It is worth noting that the associationist view of knowledge which was developed by Hume and which led into empiricism was clearly based on the pattern of Newtonian physics, although, as Kemp Smith has pointed out, Newton himself would have had no sympathy with Hume's position (op. cit., p. 71 f).

32. See especially Polanyi, *The Tacit Dimension*, 1967, Ch. 2, pp. 29 ff; *Knowing and Being*, pp. 154 ff, 216 ff, 225 ff, 233 ff.

33. For a general orientation see J.P. Sartre, *Existentialism and Humanism* (1948). The basic position is well put by Merleau-Ponty: 'Ontological contingency, the contingency of the world itself, being radical, is what forms the basis once and for all of our ideas of truth.' *Phenomenology of Perception* (1962), p. 398. Cf. P. Masterton, *Atheism and Alienation* (1971), pp. 128 ff, who offers a lucid account of this radicalization of contingency through the rejection of the Creator.

34. Sartre, *Existentialism and Humanism*, pp. 27 ff.

35. Ibid., p. 34.

36. Ibid., pp. 33, 54 f.

37. Sartre, *Being and Nothingness* (1966): see the sections of Part Two on 'Immediate Structures of the For-Itself', especially pp.128 ff.

38. *Existentialism and Humanism*, pp.41 f, 44, 47, 54 ff.

39. *Being and Nothingness*, pp.623 ff.

40. *Being and Nothingness*, p.49.

41. Ibid., p.624.

42. Ibid., Introduction, section 3, pp.9 ff. Cf. F.H. Heinemann, *Existentialism and Modern Predicament* (1953), pp.117 ff.

43. See the long discussion of transcendence and nothing in *Being and Nothingness*, pp.238 ff, and earlier p.139 f.

44. Norman Kemp Smith, *The Credibility of Divine Existence* (1967), p.376 f.

45. Duns Scotus, *Ordinatio*, prol. p.3, q.3 (n.150, 168-71) (*Opera Omnia*, ed. C. Balić, vol.i, 1950). See further, T.F. Torrance, 'Intuitive and Abstractive Knowledge from Duns Scotus to John Calvin', *De doctrina Ioannis Duns Scoti, Acta Congressus Scotistici Internationalis Oxonii et Edimburgi 11-17 Sept. 1966 celebrati*, vol.iv, *Scotismus decursu saeculorum* (1968), pp.291-305.

46. Karl Barth, *Church Dogmatics*, iii.3, p.117.

47. Cf. here the perceptive discussion by Emil Brunner of 'The depth of the distinction and interpretation of the problem of evil' in *The Mediator* (1934), pp.122-52.

48. Barth, op. cit., iii.2, p.293 f.

49. See the discussion of the mystery of evil and the nature of divine power in F.W. Camfield, *The Collapse of Doubt* (1945), chs.5-7.

50. Cf. Barth on *das Nichtige*, 'God and Nothingness', *Church Dogmatics* iii.3, pp.288-378.

51. See above, n. 40 and 54 to Ch. 2, pp.148 ff. For a recent exposition of Prigogine's concept of the thermodynamics of living organism and dissipative systems, see A.R. Peacocke, *Creation and the World of Science* (1979), pp.97 ff. For an earlier account of stable open-systems which in some measure anticipates Prigogine's thought, see Polanyi, *Personal Knowledge* (1958), pp.384 f, 402, and my account of this in 'The Open Universe and the Free Society', *Ethics in Science and Medicine*, vol.vi (1979), pp.151 ff.

52. See Polanyi, *Meaning* (1975), pp.173 ff, 182 f, for the notion of a gradient of meaning operative in evolution.

53. Cf. here the idea put forward by C.S. Lewis that the 'life-force' has somehow been corrupted, *The Problem of Pain* (1940, Fontana edit., 1957), p.123.

54. I find support for this argument in that of Polanyi, who brings information theory to bear upon the DNA chain to show that it must be an open-structure, for if the configuration of the chain were fully determined by the chemical interaction of the links, the chain would have no information content at all. Hence to say, with Crick and Watson, that the arrangement of links in a DNA chain is a bearer of information is also to say that such a chain is not ordered as a chemical compound alone but is essentially inexplicable in terms of physics and chemistry. Likewise, Polanyi argues,

the structure of living beings is characterized by the fact that its pattern is not the result of forces known to physics and chemistry. See 'Do Life's Processes Transcend Physics and Chemistry?', *Science*, vol. clx (1968), pp.1308-12; 'Life Transcending Physics and Chemistry', *Chemical and Engineering News*, vol. vl (1967), pp.54-66; 'Science and Man', *Proceedings of the Royal Society of Medicine*, vol. lxiii (September 1970), pp.970 ff. See further, *Knowing and Being*, 'Life's Irreducible Structure', ch. 14, pp.225-39; *Meaning*, pp.164 ff.

55. This would have to be formulated somewhat on the pattern of the Gödelian theorem—Kurt Gödel, *Über formal unentscheidbare Sätze der Principia Mathematica und verwandter Systeme*, in *Monatshefte für Mathematik und Physik*, 38 (1931), pp.173-98. Eng. tr. by B. Meltzer, with an introduction by R.B. Braithwaite, 1962. Gödel established that a system is consistent if no proposition can be both proved and disproved within it, and complete if every proposition formalized in terms of the system can be proved or disproved within it. What is needed is a procedure enabling us to decide whether or not any proposition formalized in terms of the system can be proved within it, but such a procedure could not be incorporated within the formal system (for we cannot make statements about propositions in a formal system within the formalization of that system), and hence we need another 'system', or 'meta-system', incorporating the precisely defined rules necessary for controlling the formalizing operations in our primary system. Although this meta-system, relative to the primary system, is not itself formalized (since it is not empty of content or assertions), that does not detract from its effectiveness in controlling the formalization of the primary system in the interest of consistency and completeness. Cf. E. Nagel and J.R. Newman, *Gödel's Proof* (1959), pp.26 ff. For Polanyi's effective use of Gödel's theorem in support of his own discussion of the relation between articulate and inarticulate, formal and informal, closed and open, systems, see *Personal Knowledge*, pp.94, 118 f, 190 ff, 259 ff, 273. He points to an analogy between the Gödelian process of innovation and the grammar of discovery outlined by Poincaré, pp.118 f, 261.

56. Richard Schlegel, 'Why can Science Lead to a Malevolent Technology?', *Centennial Review*, vol. xxi.1 (1977), pp.1-18. 'In a few summary words, we can say that the capacities for ill in the applying of science arise first in its successful method of gaining knowledge by abstracting or isolating a part of a total natural domain; then, control or interference using only the part may have unforeseen consequences, since a natural system responds as a whole and not as the part taken by science; and finally, until a few decades ago the problem of harmful technology tended to be disregarded since basic physical science supported a view which placed man out of the nature he studied, with no determination by him on the state of the natural world.' p.14. For the strange exclusion of man the

knower from the domain of nature, see also E. Schrödinger, *Mind and Matter* (1958), pp. 38 ff, 43, 66.

57. See above, p. 156, note 42.

58. W. Heisenberg, *Physics and Beyond* (1971), p. 214; cf. also pp. 10 f, 14, 33. For his concept of 'central order' see pp. 11, 14, 84, 214, 216, 241, 247.

59. E. H. Hutten, *The Origins of Science* (1962), p. 167.

60. Few modern thinkers have realized the immense gravity in the concept of *kenosis* as the incarnation of God in *contingent* existence, as D. M. MacKinnon has. See *Borderlands of Theology* (1968), pp 79 ff, and 'The Relation of the Doctrines of the Incarnation and the Trinity', in *Creation, Christ and Culture*, ed. R. W. A. McKinney (1976), p. 99.

61. Cf. the enlightening analysis of this point by St. Anselm who shows that the crucifixion of Christ was an act which 'both ought and ought not to be', but according to diverse considerations — *diversis considerationibus — De veritate, Opera Omnia*, ed. F. S. Schmitt (1938), vol. i, pp. 186–88.

62. The term *number* is used here not in any mystical sense, but neither is it used in any merely formalist or in any logicist sense separated from its objective or intuitive content. As Friedrich Waismann said, the equation $2 + 2 = 4$ stands closer to an empirical proposition than to a tautology (*Introduction to Mathematical Thinking* (1951), p. 119). It is therefore more than a statement asserting something objective about a *concept*, i.e. only indirectly related to the external world through what Frege called a 'judgment'. ('The Concept of Number', in *Philosophy of Mathematics. Selected Readings*, edit. by P. Benacerraf and H. Putnam (1964), pp. 85–112). Rather are we concerned with a physical mode of thought and not just an abstract symbol of measurement which would be to omit part of its content. Cf. Einstein's critique of Russell at this point, in his contribution to P. A. Schilpp, *The Philosophy of Bertrand Russell* (1944), pp. 279–91. This is not to confound physical reality with our measurement of it, but to reject the dualist relation between mathematics and nature, or reason and experience, which inevitably interpolates something between the object and the subject. That dualism is what Einstein sought to overcome in his more realist integration of geometry and experience.

63. No more than 'number' can 'word' be taken in a merely formalist or logicist sense, empty of its objective or intuitive content. St. Anselm showed this in his two-fold approach to 'word'. Initially he defined word (*verbum* or *nomen*) as vocable signifying reality (*vox significans rem*) — *De Grammatico 17 (Opera Omnia*, vol. i, p. 162), and *Proslogion 4* (vol. i, p. 103). However, since 'word' has its significance or truth not in itself but in the reality to which it refers, it is principally and properly what it is in relation to the reality signified, that is 'real word' (*rei verbum*) —*Monologion 10* (vol. i, p. 25). This is 'word' in its objective orientation with which

we have to do in our basic forms of thought and speech. For St.
Anselm the world which has been created by God has been given
a language of its own (*locutio rerum*) which in its creaturely form
depends on and points back to the creative Word, or the Divine
Language (*locutio apud Summam Substantiam*)—*Monologion 10*
vol.i, p.25)—it is in that correlation between the created word
and God's Word, the speech of created reality and the uncreated
Speech of God, that the created world possesses its intelligibility
and significance. See further my essay 'The Place of Word and
Truth in Theological Inquiry according to St. Anselm', in *Studia
Mediaevalia et Mariologica P. Carolo Balić OFM septuagesimum
explenti annum dicata* (1971), pp.133-60.

Index